Journeys to the Underworld

JOURNEYS TO THE UNDERWORLD

FIONA PITT-KETHLEY

Chatto & Windus

LONDON

Published in 1988 by
Chatto & Windus Ltd
30 Bedford Square
London WC1B 3RP

A CIP catalogue record for this book is available
from the British Library

ISBN 0 7011 3223 X

Photoset in Linotron Sabon by
Rowland Phototypesetting Ltd
Bury St Edmunds, Suffolk
Printed in Great Britain by
Redwood Burn Ltd
Trowbridge, Wiltshire

Contents

Introduction

As a child I was always fascinated by the story of the sibyl. At that time I only knew of the existence of one in a tale my mother had told me. An old woman of Cumae offered Tarquin, King of Rome, nine books for 300 gold pieces. He refused and she burnt three of them, offering him six for the same price. When he refused, she again burnt three books. He bought the remaining three for the full 300 gold pieces.

I realised even then that there was a profound truth hidden in the story – a lesson in salesmanship and in life. I was sometimes a lonely only child. I used to ask to play with other children and be refused. My mother told me to do something so interesting that all the other kids would beg to join me. It worked. It was another lesson that I've never forgotten.

When I was given the chance to write a travel book, I had to look for something that I could bear to find out about, something that was relevant to my life. I'm a reluctant traveller – at the first invitation I sent my editor a very long list of places I did not want to go to. When it comes down to it, I'm only interested in ruins, because the travel I like best is the travel of the mind through Time.

Few non-royal women have made it into the pages of history. The stories of the sibyls are those of the most influential women of the ancient world. Only a few facts and legends of them and their connection with the cult of the dead remain. The whole subject is surrounded by mystery. The sibyls, too, were inspired, as poets are supposed to be inspired. In examining what is known of them and what is still left of the places where they were consulted, I might come at some sort of truth about this inspiration. Yet by the end of my travels I realised that there were questions regarding them that I would never find answers to, only more questions.

I decided to go to the sibylline sites at Rome, Tivoli, Cuma, Avernus and Marsala. I would also see a little of the land of the Etruscans, who were specialists in soothsaying, and any oracular spots I came across. I would mix with and talk a lot to strangers in order to find out the local superstitions as well as those that can be read in libraries.

There are many different traditions. Some authors prefer to believe in only one sibyl, saying that she travelled from place to place – Colophon, Delos, Delphi, Erythrae, etc. But most other sources enumerate ten sibyls: the Persian, Libyan, Delphic, Cimmerian, Erythraean, Samian, Cumaean, Hellespontian, Phrygian and Tiburtine. They all had their separate books of prophecy, although some say the Sibyl of Cumae's oracles were always given orally. The Cimmerian, Cumaean and Tiburtine sibyls were located in Italy.

The Erythraean is generally thought to be the earliest. It is probably her collection that was sold to one of the Tarquins at about the end of the sixth century BC. One legend has it that this sibyl was promised as many years of life by Apollo as the grains of sand that she could collect in her hand, on condition that she never saw her native Erythraean soil again. She moved to Cuma and all went well until the Erythraeans sent her a letter with a clay seal. She looked at this fragment of soil and died. According to Ovid she was given this gift by Apollo who was in love with her. He'd offered her any wish. She forgot to ask for eternal youth though. Apollo would have given her this too if she'd slept with him. Instead, she chose to remain unmarried, living for hundreds of years. She talks of her body changing and becoming slight with age, although her voice would remain the same, 'though perceived by none, I shall still be recognised by my voice. My voice the Destinies will leave me.' (Ovid's *Metamorphoses*, translated by Henry T. Riley.) The Cumaeans used to show a coffer of brass containing her remains. The Marsalans believe that she is buried in their town. Plutarch talks, more poetically, of the sibyl becoming the face in the moon.

It's not categorically stated by the old authors that all sibyls were virgins. I think St Jerome started that one. He had a thing

2

about virgins. Sir John Floyer's translation of the amalgam known as the Sibylline Oracles contains a very unvirginal confession in the Seventh Book:

O me who am wicked! for what evils did I formerly with a design? and I did others unwillingly; I have committed whoredom many times, and I never married; I was unfaithful to all, but obliged others by a brutish oath; I shut out of my house The Poor; but walking in the porch, I admitted those who were like me, not considering the command of God; for this reason fire hath eaten me; and after this consumption I shall not live again, but an ill time will destroy me; and men shall make me a monument, but they who will come after shall throw me into the sea, with the stones that cover me, because I lay with my father, and produced for him a dear son. Let all of you cast me away, for so I shall live, and fix my eyes on heaven.

Floyer theorised that the various books in this work were written by different sibyls. 'The incest this sibyl was guilty of,' he says, 'does incline me to think she was a Persian Sibyl.' In this version, she is described variously as a daughter-in-law of Noah (nymphs were often supposed to be descended from his family), Circe's daughter, or the sister of Isis.

Virginity in either sex has often been connected with prophecy. I don't know why this should be. My second sight is still functioning undamaged. I suppose that what could spoil any dedicated vocation and lead to corruption is having ties – being concerned about a family. These days there are other alternatives to either state. Probably there always were for those who knew the right ways. Pliny hints at abortifacient or contraceptive herbs but doesn't spill the beans. If Roman witches were prepared to dig up nasty relics in the way that Horace describes, I should imagine they wouldn't have been squeamish about less revolting things. The gods would probably not have been horrified if a priestess had erred. The male priests of Hercules the Woman-Hater had to keep away from women during their period of officiation – one slipped up, but a merciful oracle was given by the god.

Being a woman alone did not always stop the sibyls from being corrupt. There is a case on record of the Delphic Sibyl taking a bribe. The briber came to a sticky end, but it's not written that *she* did.

There's a parallel to the Bride-of-Christ idea in the legend that

3

connects the original sibyl with Apollo. This idea was taken up eagerly by Christians. The sibyls were the acceptable face of paganism. In one of the earliest and most beautiful pieces of Christian writing, *The Shepherd of Hermas*, the writer has a vision while on the way to Cumae of an old woman walking and reading a book. She gives him the book to copy. He says, 'I transcribed every letter, for I found no syllables. And as soon as I had finished what was written in the book, the book was suddenly caught out of my hands, but by whom I saw not.' Later, 'a very goodly young man' appeared to Hermas in his sleep and asked:

'What thinkest thou of that old woman from whom thou receivedst the book? Who is she?' I answered, 'A sibyl.' 'Thou art mistaken,' said he, 'she is not.' I replied, 'Who is she then, Sir?' He answered me, 'It is the Church of God.' And I said unto him, 'Why then does she appear old?' 'She is therefore,' said he, 'an old woman, because she was the first of all the creation, and the world was made for her.'

The Church, throughout this book, is very much in the pattern of a sibyl. She makes a further appointment for revelations as the priestess did with Aeneas. There is a ghostly quality about the next meeting:

I observed the hours, and came into the place where I had appointed her to come. And I beheld a bench placed; it was a linen pillow, and over it spread a covering of fine linen. When I saw these things ordered in this manner, and that there was nobody in the place, I began to be astonished, and my hair stood on end, and a kind of horror seized me for I was alone.

In later literature other characters have a sibylline role – Virgil took Dante round the underworld, then Beatrice showed him purgatory. The title of sibyl could also be used to dignify and lend authenticity to prophecies. One old Scots poem begins:

Here followeth a prophecy pronounced by a noble Queen and Matron called Sibylla Regina Austri that came to Solomon through the which she compiled four books at the instance and request of the said King Solomon and others divers, and the fourth book was directed to a noble king called Baldwin, King of the broade isle of Britain.

But that's enough of literature; it was time to go and examine the sites. Before I left, I went to see my own personal sibyl, Morgana. Morgana is a 10p machine in one of the arcades in

Hastings. Over the years she has given me good value. Some paragraphs displayed on the machine tell her history:

Her image captured by a beam of light, Morgana speaks her prophecies across the vast spaces that separate her body from the life essence – a force which has been sustained electronically in order to preserve her uncanny prognostications.

Morgana's strange gift first developed at the age of 7 years when a tragic fire destroyed her parents' farmhouse near Budapest. Their lives were saved by the young child who had warned them hours before the fire broke out. Since that day, her powers became more widely recognised. Today, her disembodied image speaks its predictions for your personal entertainment.

What she told me you can see unfold in the pages of this book.

Ambassador

'Ambassador from Britain's crown,
And type of all her race.'

('The Private of the Buffs' by Sir F. H. Doyle)

Throughout my childhood my father had a lot of foreign visitors. Most thanked us on leaving and said it was nice to see how the typical English family lived. We were glad to relax when they had gone, make up rude rhymes about them and let the twelve cats out of our stinking kitchen.

As I left for Italy, I knew that I too would be making the superficial judgement that every family, every person is typical. And to them, I would always be the Englishwoman abroad. Whatever I did, or was willing to do, they would expect the next Englishwoman to do also. It was a heavy responsibility.

The English on holiday, we all know, are a more carefree lot than at home. Booze and casual sex are a must for both men and women. Football fans are expected to have the energy to be vandals as well.

I'm not a football fan. I'm not much of a boozer either. It's not that I don't like the taste. It's just that I don't make a nice drunk. The three times I got drunk, at about six-yearly intervals, I just threw up all over the floor. On each occasion I vowed to give the stuff up. A day or so later, when the fragility had passed off, I realised that moderation might be a more civilised path. Cheap wine is the thing to be avoided in my case. Spirits go down nicely with no ill effects. I never cough like the heroines in old films. The trouble with wine is that it's an unknown quantity and Château Literary Party is the worst.

Casual sex is much more in my line. I really like that and it hasn't made me throw up yet. Most women on package tours pick up the waiters at the hotel. It saves them spending time away from the beach trying to find someone else. I don't like package tours, waiters or sunbathing though. Waiters only know about food, if that, and they're a servile breed. I'm more into picking up the guides and archaeologists working on sites or in museums.

On the whole, casual sex suits me very well as a life style. I'm not exploited – I use as much as I'm being used. When the pleasure stops I can walk away. Of course, the morally inclined like to tell me that, sooner or later, I'll catch some form of VD. (I get the feeling they'd actually like me to.) Well, if I do, at least I'll have the consolation of knowing that it wasn't a friend who passed it on to me. A lot of women have caught one disease or another from their husbands or long-term lovers, and they've had to wash socks as well.

Some people like to apply the labels 'tramp', 'nymphomaniac' or 'slag' to my type of woman. In my view a tramp is a person who has no home and not many belongings – about a bagful in fact – and who likes travelling. This cannot possibly apply to me. I have a home which is dropping to pieces, several thousand books, two stray cats and two pet seagulls. That's a lot of responsibility.

I've known a few male 'tramps'. In fact, men seem more prone to the condition. I remember meeting one artist who thought he was bloody clever saving the price of a bedsit by sponging various nights' lodgings off one or other of his female friends. He worked so hard at this that he didn't get any painting done. He may have been refined and well-educated on paper, but he was definitely worthy of the description 'tramp' and he didn't get a night's lodging from me.

Nobody in his or her right mind could describe me as a nymphomaniac. I only have sex with good-looking men. That means I'm exceptionally discriminating. Some people say I ought to go further than that and only have affairs with *nice* men. I think they're being unrealistic though. I wouldn't have wanted to stay a virgin till I was due for the Queen's telegram.

'Slag' I feel doesn't really fit me either. Slags sound rather drab and unsuccessful, ill-dressed, and, worse still, *romantic*. The slag has as many affairs as me, but she believes in Love with a capital L. She ignores the evidence of her own life. She is fundamentally dishonest. It's always 'Love' with her, even when the black eyes set in. There are some men of course who could rightly be called 'slags'.

The other label that's applied to normal, healthy women who love sex is 'cheap'. I'm not cheap, I'm free. There's a world of difference.

Labels should be applied to both sexes. Sexism is not got rid of by calling a poet a poetess. 'Poetess' is and always will be mildly derogatory. There can be no such thing as a great poetess. Poets can be either sex. I intend to undermine the power of anyone who thinks otherwise.

I like to think I'm a sort of gay bachelor, Don Juan or Casanova. I don't think I ever really give men anything to complain of, so I'm one up on some in these categories. After all, I can't leave them holding the baby. Raping a man may be a nice fantasy, but it is quite impossible in its extremer forms. I never promise permanence to anyone. I believe in honesty. I wouldn't do what the average man does – seduce by lies. I don't pretend to love. I don't swear I'll be there tomorrow.

So why do I bother? Because I love sex. Food, drink, sex and money are the four great loves of my life. I thoroughly suspect any individual who says that he or she does not love all these in one shape or another. I am profoundly convinced that such a person must be either lying or suffering from some grave psychological or physical defect.

Everywhere I went in Italy I was told that it's bad to travel alone. I see no evidence for this. Travelling alone means that I can do what I want when I want. I have to fraternise all the way. Singleness is not loneliness. Travelling is like life in this respect.

My need for freedom makes the long-term relationship not all that desirable. I've avoided 9 to 5 jobs. I want my life to be one long adventure. I suppose that I must have a much lower boredom threshold than most people.

Of course, my attitude means passing most of my life without anyone I could honestly describe as a regular boyfriend. In many people's view, being without a boyfriend is a kind of disability –

something you should be either sympathised with or stigmatised for. I think this idea dehumanises women. I am angry that a woman's importance should be seen only through the man she's with. We will never attain any measure of equality while we see ourselves in this way. All the human possibilities are open to a woman. She can walk through the night, run marathons, etc. We may not be as fast or as strong yet, but we will be. Strength is only a matter of education. Of course, you can do all these things *with* a man – in theory anyway. The single woman though is a free woman, without encumbrances. She is not *more* vulnerable, she is less vulnerable. Statistics prove that married men and single women live longer. That suggests that marriage might be very bad for a woman's health. We should think twice. Perhaps we should start giving it up, like smoking.

My next-door neighbour sometimes says 'If you ever need a man . . .' offering her husband's services. Well, I can mend fuses, plaster, render, fix slates, shift heavy objects, etc. About the only thing I can't do is impregnate somebody. I'm rather glad about that. I couldn't have afforded the paternity suits.

Some old-fashioned women talk about 'needing a man' in a sexual sense. Well, I don't *need* a man . . . I fancy one though, from time to time, like I fancy a bit of chocolate or an ice cream. Italy of course is a good place to satisfy a craving for men or ice cream. Ice cream can be had in a thousand flavours, big, little, large, with or without cream on top, sometimes a tourist rip-off, sometimes good value that the locals are queuing up for.

What of Italian men? Are there such things as national characteristics? I think so. We probably aren't born with them. It's education and society that fuck us up.

There's a lot of prudishness in modern Italy. Churches have notices banning the showing of much flesh. I once saw an octogenarian in shorts turned away from St Peter's. It was a bit unrealistic of the doorkeeper. He couldn't have been much temptation to anybody. Can the tales about Catholics bathing under aprons be true? Possibly. Some Italian men have an annoying habit of wanting to be masturbated or masturbating you *through* clothing. It must do a lot for their dry-cleaning bills.

As for sex itself – they are certainly more willing than the British, but then everybody is. The Englishman is not an easy lay. It's not that he's any worse sexually, once you get him down to it. It's just that he takes a devil of a long time to get there. It's arguable whether he's worth waiting for. It's not very flattering if someone isn't sure he wants to have sex with you and needs a few drinks to pluck up the courage.

Italian men are more into sex *al fresco*. Either this proves they don't have a home to go to, or else that they do, with a wife in it. I've no objection to sex *al fresco* as long as it's a really fine day, there's some shade and the grass is soft.

Neapolitan Erections

As you come into Napoli Centrale by train you see a lot of half-built high-rise flats made of small breeze blocks with mortar oozing out between them like peanut butter. Presumably the whole will be rendered after a fashion to cover the gaps and unevennesses.

My train was two hours late, something that is quite average in Italy. All the long-distance ones manage to pick up this kind of delay along the way. The Ladies, or rather *Donne* proved a nice surprise. It was, in fact, about the only clean spot I saw in that city. I had felt my spirits sinking after the sight of those half-built surburban tenements, so it proved a palatial place to relax in. Every cubicle was about the size of a hotel bedroom, with lavatory, wash-basin and bidet. I took yards and yards of toilet-paper, as it felt like the kind puppies roll in. I knew from past holidays in Italy that this could well be the last decent sheet of the stuff I came across.

Somebody somewhere once told me that Naples was beautiful. I wonder why. There was a female leper in residence outside the left luggage office and a man who walked up and down saying: '*Sangue, sangue* . . .' I told myself stories about why he was obsessed with blood. He was a madman, I decided, intent on some Mafia-style revenge. It was days before I learned the truth about that.

I don't really fancy big hotels. Perhaps it's all my left-wing ancestors. I'd love to be rich, mainly for the freedom, but I'm sure I could never cope with others waiting on me. I don't want service or servility. I prefer the places where you carry your own bag up the stairs. There's more privacy. At that moment, too, I had a real need to save money, so I decided to do things the poor way, finding the cheapest lodgings and lunching out of paper bags a lot. I booked myself into a sufficiently disgusting *pensione* for two days – I'm cautious – and went out looking for something to eat.

I was followed at once by a pack of men. I decided, English style, to walk on, ignoring their remarks. They kept trying different languages . . . *'Parla italiano?' 'Sprechen Sie Deutsch?' 'Parlez-vous français?'* When their languages ran out they tried foods . . . *'Caffè?' 'Gelato?' 'Pizza?' 'Spaghetti?'* A completely bald dog joined in as I tried doubling up side roads. I didn't fancy sitting down outside any of the restaurants I passed, as I was perfectly certain that I would be joined for supper by six men and the bald dog.

It's better, of course, to talk to your tormentors in a case like that. A lot of the men who come up to you abroad, like the ones back home, are only after a small amount of human contact, a few questions and answers, a smile or two. Italians are a particularly nosey lot. They like to do a little market research on tourists. They are obviously all compiling psychological treatises for doctorates. Perfect strangers come up to me on stations, ask my name, profession, age, whether I'm a virgin or not, whether I've made love in Italy etc. Quite often that is all they want. They're just passing time before their train arrives.

That night I couldn't be bothered to answer those men, so I bought a rather nasty filled roll and some mineral water and headed back to my room to contemplate the sinisterly-stained bidet and the bell on the wall marked *'Cameriera'* – chambermaid.

One of the two chambermaids was like something from a James Bond movie. He was the one who did all the sheet-folding. He wore a vest and had immensely strong-looking, muscular arms and a completely bald head which came to a sort of point. The other one was small. He slept a lot on a bench in the corridor in front of a television. He had styes on his eyes and looked very old. He really hated me. I could tell by the look in his eyes every time I asked to use the shower. As it was a cheap hotel, I had to get the top of the tap for this from whoever was on duty. Every time I asked for it he said: *'Ora?'* (Now?) with a look of incredulity. When I handed it back it was *'Ha finito?'* (Have you finished?) with a sneer that said why the fuck did you bother if you were only going to take five minutes. He was nearly as pleasant as the fat woman in the nearby bank.

The proprietor had a split palate and spoke Italian as a snake would. He was also tone deaf, but this didn't stop him singing a lot. The sound reminded me vaguely of a seal I once heard ululating up a rocky cleft on a wild stretch of the Pembrokeshire coast. It was so horrible I started listening out for it.

Neapolitans, I decided, are supremely unattractive. They didn't look any better by the morning light. One of them told me that all the locals are '*molto gentili*'. It's nice to learn new foreign expressions when you're abroad. *Molto gentili* I found pretty soon must mean that they put their hands up your skirt and want to fuck you in some uncomfortable place. Physically, they look like the rather overweight models used by Neoclassical painters such as David. They all have wide waists, muscular bums, large cocks and tiny finger-nails. You can't help noticing the cocks because they rest their hands on them. They have an attitude far from that shown in a remark in Hugo Williams's *No Particular Place to Go*. They would not dream of describing their erections as a 'painful head of sperm'. Instead, when they get one, they nudge their friends in the bus, church or wherever, point to it and start screaming with laughter. Then, they pat its head as if to say 'Good boy!' and rest their right hand on it to make sure that all the women in the place notice. I had to sit opposite one of these on the train from Turin to Naples. He had even put his feet up on the head rest and gone to sleep, twisted towards me like an inverted odalisque in an invisible hammock. I assumed he was an atypical weirdo, till I met the rest.

In the morning, Naples looked a shade less sinister. Most of the market stalls had disappeared. Some of the black street-traders only seem to operate at night, like the one who sells used leather at 5000 lire a garment. I had felt quite tempted by his stall, but, although the jackets *looked* big and butch on the outside, they were only about thirty-two inches on the inside. Besides, buying used leather at night seems a bit bent. What would I do if I found bloodstains on it when I looked at it by morning light?

I intended to head for Sicily the following evening, so I went to the docks to buy my ticket for the ferry. On my way out of the customs' gates, an old man dropped his trousers, bent over and showed me his striped boxer shorts. He was surrounded by a group of other old men, laughing and encouraging him. Probably it's a deadly Neapolitan insult they offer tourists in this part of town. A lot of Italians seem to resent outsiders, believing that they have vastly more money. I felt this same hatred when I changed travellers' cheques in the Banca del Lavoro. They won't let you cash them before ten there, and when they give you the money they literally throw it at you. It's quite amusing, because the small coins just bounce back off the glass and cause them more trouble in the long run.

I started sampling churches on my way to the little station for the towns west of Naples. I awarded prizes mentally for images. Those in Santa Maria delle Grazie looked potential winners, I thought at first. They are life-size and in full dress like waxworks, enclosed in glass cases with gilded ornamentations. At the feet of the saints there are little silver images of women and babies, artificial flowers, embroidered hankies and photographs. Then I came upon San Giovanni Evangelista. In a case with what looks like a Joseph and Child, there are silvered tin embossed hands and feet, also three relief figures – a female one in a dress, an effeminate male one with slight breasts and a loin-cloth, and one of a man in a suit. Modern suits never come across well in sculpture. Every time I see a statue in trousers I can't help laughing. An old woman nearby turned round to watch in the midst of her prayers, leaving her mouth and the hand on her rosary on automatic pilot. I hadn't actually started laughing, but I could feel the corners of my mouth twitching, so I got out and left her to her devotions.

It was a very devout time of the year for Naples. I was there just two weeks before one of the tri-annual liquefactions of the blood of St Januarius. There were notices everywhere telling people that this was a time for prayer, purification and regeneration. Meetings and pray-ins were advertised all over the city. I got nabbed several times by women selling tracts connected with these. I very happily trotted out my 'Non capisco. Sono inglese.' I always say I don't understand when people want my money abroad. Maybe I should pretend to be a lost Italian with the Jehovah's Witnesses back home. At least the Neapolitan text-carriers took my being English as a valid excuse for not giving.

Of course the city used to have even more relics. Here is an account of them from the seventeenth-century traveller Misson's *A New Voyage to Italy*:

They keep at St Lewis of the Palace, a considerable quantity of Virgin's milk, which becomes liquid on all Our Lady's festivals. At St John Carbonnara, the blood of St Januarius boils up when one puts it near the shrine in which his body is kept; and the blood of St John Baptist, which is at St Maria Donna Romita, makes a like ebullition too, while they are saying the mass of the beheading of the Saint. I will say nothing of the pieces of the true Cross, the nails, the branches of the Crown of Thorns, the Images of the Virgin made by St Luke, nor an infinity of such like rarities, whose number would tire both you and me. At St Dominick Major you may see the Crucifix, which said one day to St Thomas Aquinas, '*Bene scripsisti de me, Thoma, quam ergo mercedem accipies?*' – Thou hast written well of me, Thomas, What reward wilt thou have?

Misson then goes on to describe quite a few more crucifixes and images which held conversations. Even a Christ that bled and laid its hand on the wound when 'struck with a ponyard'. The cloister of the convent of the Carthusians contained the 'famous crucifix of Michelangelo, drawn, as it is said, after the life, from a certain peasant whom that painter crucified for that purpose.'

I felt a certain amount of disrespect creeping into my lapsed Protestant heart when I viewed the cathedral. *Il Duomo* is in better taste than the other churches – quite good paintings set in a thirteenth-century building. My only trouble in there was with the Chapel of San Gennaro, a crypt beneath the main altar. This holds the blood of St Januarius, a sort of Christian oracle you might say. Do they *have* to keep it in a beer barrel though? There's something intensely ludicrous about the sight of a fourteen-inch keg set with great reverence in a glass case.

This building was probably much nicer when it was a Temple of Neptune. Pagan shrines are in much better taste than Christian ones. That seems like a very good reason for being pagan instead, if you must be anything. Besides, it is so obvious to anyone of any intelligence that the world is run by a committee.

San Gennaro's barrel reminds me strongly of one I saw being used by *The Drinking Bear* in the penny arcade on Southend Pier when I was a mite. It's also a bit like a larger version of a prop from one of those *Miser's Dream* machines. I wished I could put a coin in it to make something happen. I quite like the candle machines in some Italian churches. 50 lire in and a light goes on (or not) for St Anthony. I once had an amazing display – a sort of *son et lumière* – when I put my coin in one of these in the Divine Love shrine outside Rome. Everything went on . . . and off . . . and on . . . and off . . . and on again. I took it as a very good omen.

San Gennaro's blood first liquefied when St Severus brought it into Naples in the time of Constantine. It does it again on the first Saturday in May in the Church of Santa Chiara, from whence it is carried in solemn procession to the cathedral so that it can do it again on the saint's death date – September the 19th – and the date of an eruption – December the 16th. The speed with which this happens provides a good or bad omen for the ensuing year.

Publius Faustus Januarius was born on a Saturday in April, 272 AD. (I have read a devout Italian book on the subject, so I know.) His father, Stefano, was of a Roman family. His mother, Teonoria Amato, was a Neapolitan. Januarius was their only son. While he was in his mother's womb he had the charming habit of jumping for joy every time she abandoned herself to prayer in a church. He was very precocious. When he was only nine months old, at the Feast of the Passion, he waved his rosy little hands as if he wanted to give alms to the poor. He used to go off alone to pray to an image of Mary at the age of five. As a child he'd take things from the house to give away – money, clothes and bread. One day, he embraced a barefoot wounded girl (just as a brother) and she turned into Christ in his arms. Christ promised to repay him.

From then on Januarius got even more pious. He started to visit imprisoned Christians. He took them food and medicine, kissed them, then buried them piously. He also rounded up all the local kids, babies even, took them down the catacombs and preached a sermon. He told them all about the Christian martyrs until they were palpitating with emotion and crying. (I was sent to a psychologist for much less at that kind of age.)

One day he had a celestial vision while he was there of a spring garden filled with roses, lilies and violets – beautifully perfumed ones – in which the King of Heaven appeared. The angel who kept the garden offered the Lord some of these flowers. The Lord said that he would give these to J. one day and that his body would rest in that cemetery. When the saint came to, he heard a voice

17

telling him that he would offer the Lord the lilies of his chastity, the violets of a bishopric and the red roses of martyrdom.

He turned ascetic after this, got pains in the head, was cured by the Virgin, started a hospital, etc. The hospital was in his old home, near the temple of Castor and Pollux. He used to carry the sick there on his shoulders. His mother helped in the wards, leaving him free to exorcise demons and raise the dead. He also wrote a book against heretics.

When his father died he provided honourably for his mother and sister Agatha and gave the rest to the Church. In 302 he was offered a bishopric, which he refused twice through Christian humility. On the third offer he accepted one in Benevento, a place which has also some interest in his relics.

Januarius's habit of prison-visiting eventually caused his downfall. He was denounced as a Christian to the Pro-consul Timothy when he went to see his cousin Sossio who was gaoled at Pozzuoli.

In common with many other saints, Januarius was hard to put down. He sang in the furnace and blew the flames back so that they caught the spectators. Various tortures failed to touch him. His mother, having less faith than him, dreamed that he was being martyred and died from grief.

Six Christians rode from Nola to join Januarius in martyrdom in the arena, but he calmed the lions etc. with the sign of the cross — something that greatly affected the 5000 pagans in the audience. (Maybe they asked for a refund on the tickets.) Finally, decapitation worked. It usually does in stories about saints and witches. Even at this stage there was another miracle. An old beggar gave the saint a piece of his hankie which Januarius promised to return later. The soldiers taunted the old man about this, but he was able to show them his bloody hankie as delivered by the spirit of the saint. Presumably it became a relic. After this there were omens — the Pro-consul became ill and the Solfatara quaked. The people from various towns came and claimed the bodies of their saints. I have a tiny fragment from St Eutychius who was, if I am not mistaken, one of the seven martyred and hailed from Pozzuoli. I mentioned this relic in a poem, 'The Ecumenical Movement'.

As well as St Januarius's body, his blood was collected and put into two ampoules. One contained the more limpid stuff, the other was full of blood that had mixed with the dust. The body went

18

through many changes of residence. From the Solfatara, where the execution took place, it was taken to the catacombs in a solemn procession. In the fifth century the head was shifted to the cathedral. In the ninth, the Beneventans stole the body and various miracles occurred when it arrived in their city. From the thirteenth to the fifteenth century it rested at the monastery of Montevergine. After that, it was reunited with the other bits in Naples.

A number of lucky escapes were attributed to the presence of the relics. Naples, it seems, was saved from countless earthquakes, tremors and eruptions, the Goths, the Vandals, plagues and cholera. The colour and quality of the blood varied from miracle to miracle. Sometimes it was bright red, sometimes blackish. It could be runny as water or thick and heavy. Sometimes it rises up. It can take anything from a few minutes to an hour to change. The Italian authority on the subject stated that it was not true that people insult the saint by telling him to turn it yellow or green if it's slow. Failure to liquefy always coincides with an epidemic, a war or cataclysm.

Saintly intervention has provided a lot of lucky escapes. A seventeenth-century English merchant wrote a letter on the 1688 earthquake in Naples. The archbishop of nearby Benevento, he said, 'was pulled out half dead from under the ruins of his palace; and there had never been a bit of him seen together again, if it had not been for the intercession of St Philip of Neri, his patron.' One curious result of this earthquake was that all the 'Belles Marguerites' – the courtesans – repented and married their gallants.

For me, the most enjoyable miracle connected with St Januarius concerns his marble bust in a chapel in Pozzuoli. A Saracen knocked the nose off this with his sword and chucked the piece in the sea. A year later, a fisherman of Baia thought he was pulling in a heavy net, but only this tiny fragment came up. He threw it back. His catch was repeated three times so he took the piece to an old priest who told him that he had found San Gennaro's nose. A great crowd went to the church and the piece was stuck back on without the aid of glue.

A more sinister miracle is that of how the saint took the plague of 1656 on himself when his remains were carried in procession from the Solfatara to the amphitheatre. A mark appeared on the neck and grew from the size of a walnut to that of a fish. Then, the yellowish bubo burst with a smell of smoke and burning.

I'd had enough of modern religion after viewing the keg, so I made my way to the Monte Santo station to take the funicular railway. There are lots of stalls nearby selling kinds of shellfish I couldn't even begin to recognise. Fish have such subtle colours that displays of them don't revolt me in the way that a butcher's shop can. For revoltingness, it would be hard to beat the barbaric shop-windows in this area. These are stocked with tripe, pinky-grey heads of bulls (or something) on fake turf under running water. The heads are spaced alternately with heaps of entrails and halves of lemons. I doubt if such piles of guts have been seen in Britain since the Middle Ages. Quite obviously these are the ingredients for the worst type of Ancient Roman black puddings. A few recipes have come down through the ages.

In a nearby backstreet, Dottore Basilio Mele (Basil Apples) offers operations without pain.

'Grandmama, What Large Teeth You Have'

If, Oppianus, you're not tempted by
Etruscus' baths, unbathed you'll surely die.
No other waters offer such allure,
Not even Aponus, which young girls abjure,
Phoebus, mild Sinuessa, Passer's streams,
Anxur the splendid, Baiae's peerless streams.
There, over all a stainless radiance plays,
And the long daylight endlessly delays,
Purple-streaked Phrygian, yellow Libyan, green
Laconian marble – all to advantage seen;
The sweating onyx with the heat suspires,
And the rich snakestone glows with subtle fires.
Too hot? Then, should the Spartan method seem
More pleasing, plunge into the natural stream
Of Marcia, or the Virgin – baths so fair
One sees white marble not the water there.
You've hardly heard all this! You don't attend –
I really fear you'll die unbathed, my friend.

(Martial, *Epigrams*, Book VI no. 42, translated by O.
   Pitt-Kethley)

The funicular railway from Naples to the towns in the Phlegrean (or burning) Fields seemed to be driven by a maniac. There are no timetables or maps in the station and the trains start upstairs. I tried asking for Cuma – after all, the railway's called the *Ferrovia Cumana* – the Cumaean Railway. The man at the desk gave me a ticket marked Torregàveta and told me to get off at Fusaro.

Inside the train there was a tiny map situated above eye level in the centre of the carriage. The names of the stations were written in red on a sand-coloured background for the land, or a blue one for the sea. Reading them was almost impossible. Before the train moved off I started to copy the names of the stops. There appeared to be two lines – the one I was going on and a second returning by another route from Torregàveta. This other line was called the *Circumflegrea*. I had just about finished my list when the train hurtled off, throwing everyone from side to side. The ride started through a tunnel glistening with black encrustations and dripping water. I soon realised that station after station had lost its name, or part of it. The whole journey became a sort of crossword puzzle or guessing game. Could o   o v. E. be Corso Vittorio Emmanuele, I wondered. Some of the stations on the map had been closed down completely too, so tourists couldn't even count their way to a stop. That summer they were having the line up between Bagnoli and Gerolomini. On this trip and my few following ones I had to bus this section. Each time the thing was handled differently. Sometimes the bus was waiting meekly outside the station, other times it was parked a street or two away and everyone did a quick sprint for it.

The bus wound along the coast past piles of vast granite blocks thrown up in lieu of a beach. There were a few men sunning their torsos on these slanting table-sized slabs by the edge of the water.

In Gerolomini, the train that shuttles back and forth for the last stage was waiting. The nearby stations of Arco Felice, Lido Augusto and Montenuovo seemed to have disappeared without trace. The train stops next at Lucrino. There's no nameboard, but the large lake tells you where you might be. Then comes Baia – you can see ships and part of a port here. Before I realised where I was the train had reached the end of the line. I had missed the unmarked Fusaro and the stop of Silenia had disappeared completely.

There is little in Torregàveta beside a restaurant or two and a beach full of black sand. I swam here, taking care not to get impaled on the anchors of small fishing boats. The water seems to be shallow for a long way out. It's more buoyant than the Channel, so the lack of depth doesn't matter much. I seemed to be able to float or swim there with the ends of my bob unsullied. The water smelt quite odd – rather sulphurous. I thought that I would be in dire need of a shower afterwards, but I was wrong. When my skin was dry it smelt perfumed. All the water along this coast has this strange quality. It is also remarkably healing. Blisters and small scratches vanish overnight after a bathe there.

From Torregàveta there are buses on to Monte Procida or back to Baia. I opted for Baia. I remembered reading of the palaces beneath the sea. A friend who's a classics professor had told me that this was the most beautiful beach in the world. There are also excavations there.

When I got on the bus I first experienced the new system which operates in most of the towns of Italy. The driver gestured to where I should buy a ticket. Inevitably I chose the wrong building and got one for the train from the station. The driver got out, had this changed for me and refunded 100 lire. The people outside Naples are far kinder than those of the city.

The bus went through a lot of hilly land and small towns. You could see the sea most of the way. It seemed a longer, less anonymous journey than in the hurtling train. Eventually I got to Baia. The main beach proved to be a dock with slimy green algae where the water lapped. Maybe there's some more charismatic beach to the north or the south, but I didn't find it that day. Somewhere along this stretch a statue of Venus was dug up – twice life size, with a globe in its right hand and oranges in the left. There was a large ruin near the dock, some Roman baths. It was shut off behind big gates and iron railings. The interior was full of luxuriant weeds. A large rat picked delicately through a carton of food by the entrance.

I took a left turn off the main coastal road after this – the Via di Sella di Baia. A long flight of steps took me past a collapsing house to the entrance of an archaeological park. This is tucked away where you could easily miss it. To the right, before you enter this, there are a few ruins mixed up with allotments. At the top of these there's a wild fig tree growing down to the ground and some vines sprawling in an untended state. I took a few of the figs as they looked like nobody's property. The air was fragrant from big bushy spearmint plants.

After this, I entered the site opposite. Archaeological parks seem

23

to be a feature of Italy – vast conglomerations of ruins, often unlabelled, mixed up with countryside or gardens. I could hardly decipher this one at first. There are countless sections of brick ruin and little flights of steps leading up or down to other levels. Broken pillars lie scattered on every side. The ruins cover a large area of hillside. They run across in tiers like ramparts. While you're on one of these levels it's hard to imagine what the whole thing could look like. I ate an apple as I walked across the highest part. I soon noticed that I was being observed by a man on a lower level. I was going to chuck my core into the abyss below. Instead, ever conscious of my nation's reputation, I parked it discreetly beneath a myrtle bush.

On the next level I met the man who'd been watching me. He told me he was a friend of the guide at the gate and that he often showed visitors round. Most of the men who work or loiter on sites are after sex, often a peculiar form. I can't say I've come across any National Trust perverts or British Museum guards equivalent to these. The most I've found in London was a cranky one in the Egyptian Room who uttered dire warnings when I drew a sketch of the casket of a particularly lethal princess. (On my way home, the tube to Ealing Common filled with smoke which made me feel for all of two minutes that the power of the Pharaohs might not be quite dead.)

I was quite glad to have someone to tell me what was what in this maze. I had read of the classical Baiae, the greatest thermo-mineral plant of Roman times, a sort of spa-city frequented by the rich and powerful. Volcanic activity had greatly altered the place though. The imperial villas, the old shore line and most of the hot-water springs had been submerged by the changes of level in the land. Only imposing ruins remain. Parts of these have been used as farmhouses, cisterns and cellars in the hillside. The section I was in, though, has been thoroughly excavated over the last four decades.

At the bottom there was the ruin of a small theatre where mythical and erotic pieces were put on as well as declamations and concerts. The higher levels contain what my guide described as *saunas*. The guides tend to talk in an updated, slangy way. It's far south of Rome, so no one round here speaks English. He talked vividly as if he could still see the Romans bathing, sweating, scraping and relaxing in these small dusty, ruined rooms. I was reminded of my time working as an extra on *Superman II*. One of the assistant directors there had that same enthusiastic naivety as he described the intergalactic villains that only he could see fighting in the air above us.

As I was led from *sauna* to *sauna* tiny remains of stucco decoration and one or two minute fragments of frescoes were pointed out to me. Almost everything had been destroyed by the saltness of the air. Eventually my guide led me into a large roofed room with an earth floor. That and the decorated rooms were part of the complex belonging to the Baths of Venus, he said, and that particular bit was where the Romans used to make love.

I began to see where his thoughts were tending. It's not often you get the chance to do it exactly where the poshest Romans did it. The Caesars might have done it here, Antony and Cleopatra, Virgil, Horace, Martial . . . who knows who – a positive *Burke's Peerage* of antiquity. Of course, *maybe* they preferred the privacy of their villas, a mile or so away. With Romans though, that might not have been the case. Now how could this perfect stranger have guessed I have a kink about sex in historic locations? (I once had it off in the Coliseum.) When in Baia do as the Romans did. I hadn't known him long, but . . . well . . . he had nice eyes.

Making love in Italy comes in two extreme forms. (For the middle range you have to stay in Britain.) There are two types of Italian men – one does it so quickly you feel like saying, 'Was that it?' The other likes to go on for hours and try various positions. They are obediently kinky and often vacillate between orifices saying: '*Qua o qua?*' (Here or here?) This antechamber to the Baths of Venus, or whatever the place was, had lots of ledges, window-sills, etc. which could prove useful.

The second type of lover seems to be trying to prove something about Italians in general. They're promoting a slogan like our *Buy British*. They usually start by asking '*Ha fatto amore in Italia?*' (Have you made love in Italy?) If you say yes, they then proceed to ask if you've made love in such and such a town – wherever you happen to be. My guide was true to form. You get the odd sex word taught you too, like *cazzo* for a prick or fucking. This comes in useful when you're eavesdropping. It's surprising how often such words crop up in commuter conversation.

When I and my guide had made full use of the ledges, he made a most bizarre request. I've met some strange men in my time, but never before had I encountered one that wanted me to sink my teeth into his cock. I always thought that was one of their darkest nightmares – the sort of thing guaranteed to send them home screaming to their *maters* or *madres* as the case might be. At the time I was wearing a rather impressive mother-of-pearl necklace – five Chinese gambling chips mounted on a strong rhodium chain. It had been strung together for me by a Spiritualist. My guide had told me previously that he liked it and that it reminded him of teeth. (Some teeth!) Little did I know the dark passions I was arousing when I bit into that apple among the ruins of Baia. I had a brainwave – I made him a happy man with the aid of my necklace and there wasn't even a snake around to suggest it.

After this interlude my guide became business-like again and showed me the rest of the ruins – the places where the dancers and actors lodged by the theatre. On the higher levels, in part of the baths, water still ran beneath a sort of bridge. In the spring, I was told, it was hot and bubbling, too hot to touch in fact. Nearby, there was a large impressive temple. It was one of those that get the name *truglio* (trough) locally from their domed mixing-bowl shape. Archaeologists insist that these were only baths, not temples, but the local traditions go on. This one is designated a Temple of Mercury in the books, but my guide called it the Temple of Diana. It is a vast dome with a circular hole in the centre. Apart from a small standing area by the entrance, the rest is filled with water like a swimming pool. The building has a most powerful echo if you stamp or speak by the water's edge. The central hole casts a perfect image of the sun on the side wall. *If* this was truly a Temple of Diana, I must have committed an appalling desecration by washing something off my hands in the water.

Whose are these temples? It's hard to tell now all their statues have been moved to museums, or bought by private collectors. Traditions differ vastly on their dedications. A map I looked at afterwards showed the ruined building near the shore, the one with the rat, as the Temple of Venus. Perhaps I'd been had, as they say. Archaeologists are rarely content to state both sides of a case. They always have to come down firmly – over firmly – on one side or the other. One book I read on these particular excavations, written by the man who had started them, stated that these ruins were not baths at all, but a vast religious complex connected with Cumae a few miles away and used for a complicated mystery initiation. This writer had spent years crawling up and down passages filled with scorpions and even got his friend to dive and take unclear underwater pictures in a very hot underground river which they were certain must be the Styx. Some men get their kicks in very funny ways.

I'm rather inclined, though, to think my teeth-fetishist friend was right about the temple being dedicated to Diana. A funny coincidence convinces me. Baedeker's *Southern Italy* says that women used to offer to dance the tarantella here for tourists. The tarantella was a dance sacred to the witch-queen Diana. (Diana, with Herodias, was considered a queen of the witches in later Italian folklore.) These days of course there are no women dancing here, or perhaps they emerge for male tourists still, leaving odd guides to do the honours for passing female ones.

There is much in Italian folklore that carries with it a memory of the old gods – Roman or Etruscan. Roman mythology is too often merged with Greek in books. The Etruscan element is rarely taken into consideration. The rhyming charms used by Italian witches frequently invoked the help of spirits with names very similar to those of the old gods. I don't know whether people use these spells now. I would guess that a few do. They were certainly still using them at the end of the last century according to C. G. Leland the antiquary's researches.

On my way to the exit of the park I was given a sprig of myrtle. Italian men love giving you sprigs of things. I usually seem to lose these, however sentimentally I intend to press them in Bibles or whatever. Myrtle is extremely fragrant when fresh. A few bushes scented the whole area. Virgil mentions myrtle growing in the section of the Elysian Fields reserved for lovers. The nearby area just outside Baia used to be shown to tourists as the Elysian Fields. Now it's just scrub and weeds though. Myrtle has a very sexy smell. It certainly beats after-shave. I think my guide must have been rolling in it, like my cats in the herb-border. His whole body smelt of it.

We said goodbye at the gate. I refused a further date, if that was

27

what you could call it. Casual sex should be kept casual. I got the statutory Italian parting pat on the bum.

For once, I did manage to hang on to my sprig. I found it in the bottom of my case when I got home. I have it still, though the smell has faded to a faint tinge of curry. I keep it now in a tin box of love letters from a bastard. It's a subtle way of feeling unfaithful to someone who let me down badly.

I caught the train back to Naples. There was another frantic rush at Gerolomini. The bus left me lost in the backstreets of Bagnoli, looking for the station. When in doubt in Italy, I look for a crone. Crones have usually been around long enough to know a thing or two. Old men never learn. They are usually too busy fancying that young girls love them and being terribly surprised when they find out they only love their money. I was directed up the hill and down a subway by the first crone I picked. Here I found an excellent tap carrying cold, clear, good water. There was quite a queue for it including a child covered in measles which I hoped I wouldn't catch. I'm a very thirsty person who can't take much sun, so I have to go around well-covered and drink all day in order to avoid sunstroke.

A Big Heart

In the morning I took my bag to the left luggage office, giving the leper a wide berth. Italian left luggage offices are much better than English ones – you pay when you collect and can leave things there for days or even months.

I headed for the Museo Archaeologico Nazionale. This has one of Italy's best collections of ancient statues and erotic postcards. Most of the statues, frescoes and mosaics came from nearby Pompeii and Herculaneum. The postcards are mainly reproductions of frescoes which are not in the museum. Somebody on the bookstall evidently has exotic tastes.

The museum is a large sixteenth-century building with inner courtyards filled with palm trees and second-class statues. The first-class statues are all over the ground floor – some are colossal. The gods most often represented seem to be Venus and Apollo, my two favourites. There are also a lot of chewed-up statues of humans labelled *Torso Virile*. These have absolutely no prick and very little in the way of balls – half a one at most.

One of the wings of the museum contains an Egyptian collection – some of which came from Pompeii. It's nice to know that somebody there had a mummy of a crocodile round the place. It must have been an interesting talking-point at Roman orgies. Unfortunately everything in this collection is set out in an over-educational manner, with lots of printed verbal diarrhoea pasted on orange hessian panels. I wonder if this place is going to end up like the buggered-up bits of the British Museum. It's sad to see that the rot has set in, even in Italy.

There are some marvellous things in this section, once you get away from the printed lectures. I liked best the small fresco panels with depictions of scenes from the Egyptian cults once in favour with fashionable Romans. One odd thing I noticed in this collection – some of the words on the labels of these cult-paintings were added in hand-written Greek, stuck in incongruously amongst the typed Italian. There was no good reason for it. The Greek words were common ones, like that for a prophet. It seemed as if someone was trying to add confusion – make things more esoteric. It's like the conflicting advice I received every time I asked how to get to the Sibyl's Cave.

On the upper floor there's another educational area – all modern – on the history of Naples. I went through this like lightning. Nearby, more in my line, there's a wonderful collection of mosaics, framed and hung on the wall. Most of these come from Pompeii. My favourite has a small fierce little tabby cat biting into a partridge on a shelf above two ducks – one with a flower in its beak – some songbirds and a few fish. The whole thing is very ambiguous, almost surreal in quality. The birds look rather alive, yet what are they doing just sitting there? Even the fish are gaping apprehensively. In the middle of the bottom shelf there are various shellfish. One of the little birds is picking at these. It all looks a bit much for the contents of a small kitchen cupboard.

Near this, there is a cruder, less subtle mosaic with fewer colours. Two cocks are about to fight in front of a stool which contains a palm, a bag of money and a staff with a double serpent – the emblem of Aesculapius. All the animal mosaics seem laden with symbolism in this way. I often think that Roman art is at its finest in the treatment of animals. There's generally a liveliness and humanity in the depiction of earthly things. The Greeks of course were better at the divine.

Roman mosaic is a wonderfully fluid form. The technique of laying a bed of it is described in detail in Pliny's *Natural History*. It's surprising, with all the complications involved, that the end results can contain such variety. The sort of thing that passes for mosaic in England – in subways and so on – had led me to believe that it could not possibly be a medium for great art before I visited Italy. There are a few Roman mosaics in England, but they are poor things. Perhaps the finest artists didn't feel like coming over and putting up with the British climate.

There are many more beautiful animal mosaics in this museum – doves, doves and parrots drinking from bowls, a panther, a whole selection of sea fish. This last looks rather like a fishmonger's advert. Some of these ones reminded me of Victorian pictorial tiling for dairies. The Victorians copied the Romans in almost everything except being civilised about sex.

There's one very large mosaic panel which is definitely not a shop sign. It's a vast battle scene – eighteen feet by nine. It has been badly damaged. Some say it is of Alexander. The central warrior has a portrait of Medusa on the front of his armour. Facially, he could bear a slight resemblance to the very beautiful portrait bust in the Capitoline Museum. He's not a real looker though – of course, some people look much worse in colour. There are times when I'm glad I can only afford a black and white TV.

The last mosaic I looked at was a vivid one of some street musicians. This was brought from Cicero's villa at Pompeii. The figures were all short, ugly and exceptionally evil-looking. In fact, they seem to bear a remarkable resemblance to many of the men and women on the streets in Naples today.

Downstairs in the Egyptian-Pompeiian section on my way to the postcards, one of the curators started drawing my attention to various panels and ancient musical instruments. He kept asking 'Ti piace?' (Do you like it?) He was using the familiar form, so I knew he meant business. He thought I was Venetian, he said, because of the lacy blouse I was wearing. I took this as a compliment, as I hadn't been to Venice at that juncture. Venetian sounded like a nice thing to be. I felt very pleased with my new pick-up, because he was the only attractive man I'd seen in Naples – dark and romantic-looking, and not overweight. Obviously he hailed from somewhere else. He was deeply impressed when he found out I'm a poet. Everybody's moved by that in Italy. (If I tell people I'm one over here, they usually say, 'I couldn't stand Poetry at school!' Or worse, the really hardened ones recite an unfunny limerick and boast it's the only poem they know.)

Antonio shook my hand and told me what an honour it was to meet me. He then looked down the front of my lacy blouse and whispered that I had 'un gran cuore' (a big heart). You need a big heart to be able to write poetry, he said. Well, I can't argue with that. He seemed very disappointed to find that I was going to Sicily that evening and gave me his phone number to ring him when I got back. It would be a great honour for him, he said.

I was greatly impressed by all this politeness. Back home, men usually let me know what a big honour it is for me going out with them. I took Antonio's number eagerly and made a mental note not to lose this one. I decided to phone him the evening of the day I got back to Naples. I thought I might even keep myself pure for him, the next few days. I rather felt I ought to keep myself pure in Sicily anyway. I'd heard such terrible things about Sicilian men. My mother had told me a tale about one to put me off: a bridegroom painted his cock green in order to test whether his young bride had ever seen a normal-coloured one. When she laughed, he killed her. I promised my mother that I would keep a straight face if I should see any green ones in Sicily.

My friends were no better than my mother. One warned me that the Mafia would force me into a shotgun marriage if I took up with a Sicilian. Another friend said that they're all so romantic and naive that I might have trouble with some sentimental soul taking me too seriously. Men never take me seriously, I told her. Still, it is a fact that it was in Sicily that pastoral poetry was invented.

Before I left the museum I bought a lot of postcards. It was a problem finding respectable ones. The bookstall stocks ones of Polyphemus fucking Galatea with a ram watching, a nymph and satyr about to, a garden fountain in the shape of Priapus, Priapus weighing his bulbous knee-length prick in a pair of scales, a couple doing it in what looks like rather an uncomfortable position for the woman – one leg and an arm round the bloke's neck, the other leg down on the couch, etc. I thought about sending my editor a picture of Pan doing something to a goat, but the three graces seemed more appropriate. My old schoolfriends got Priapic lampstands and I kept the other pictures for my private collection.

My next task was to get to the docks with my bag. I walked, which was a bad idea. Once I got through the main entrance it was a long way across strange deserted tram tracks. I lost a purse of small change somewhere, but it wasn't worth going back. It was probably months before anyone found it in that strange emptiness.

The Tirrhenian offices, where the boat leaves for Palermo, are like a shopping precinct inside. There were lots of over-priced souvenirs – coral, cards, guide books in four languages. Curiously, there was a second-hand bookshop mixed up in the middle of all this, with strange items like *Memorie di un Depravato* in the 'Psicopatico' section. This had a silhouette of the depraved hero on the dust-jacket, but he didn't look any worse than the locals. I resisted the temptation to buy it.

Instead, I went to the *Donne*, which was full of old men and unflushed lavatories, then slumped on a bench to wait for the boat. There were three fat Italian boys opposite, sleeping with their hands on their erections. Two English hikers turned up next. Then came a bossy Italian tour guide who wanted to round us up because her clients hadn't appeared yet. She reminded me of a sheepdog. Last of all, a vast band of religious teenagers rolled up and started to wail choruses to the accompaniment of a single guitar played badly by a pious fifteen-year-old in frayed denim shorts. All these unattractive, unmade-up teenage Italian girls – it was obviously a bloody pilgrimage. I was seriously relieved to find out that the party was bound for Tunisia.

When the gates opened there was a mad rush for the ferry. We all ran with our bags in one hand, an embarkation visa flapping in the other. Once on board I battled to the TV lounge and won part of a sofa for the night.

I'd expected a wonderful view of sunset over the Bay of Naples as we left, but the ship was well closed in. I don't think they allow any landlubbers on deck. You can't see much but a little sky through the tiny portholes, so I concentrated on watching TV to improve my Italian. I caught the tail end of a Japanese movie – four men in dressing gowns, bashing each other. 'Hi-ya' is the same in any language. After that came the adverts. Three chefs stuck their hands in the Mouth of Truth while saying they have the best virgin olive oil in Italy. (One legend says that Virgil made the *Bocca della Verità* as a test for women's chastity – something I shouldn't have imagined he'd have cared very much about.)

The News in Italian is much more melodramatic. The cameras zoom in suddenly and crazily on victims and blood. It all reminded me of the Sacred Hearts back in the Neapolitan churches. Much of the rest of the evening was taken up by sport and everyone crowded into the lounge to watch the boxing match. An American and an Italian were fighting for a title. I got the impression that the audience might be looking for an American to murder if the wrong man won. Did they know the difference between American and British, I wondered. Luckily the Italian made it by a knockout and everyone was happy.

After Cycling and more News, it was time for the late film – *Love Story*. The title was left untranslated. Ali McGraw sounds even more of a pain in the arse in Italian. She kept calling Ryan O'Neal '*Carogna*' (swine) – a word I must remember to use more often. A pregnant woman rushed out to be sick about five minutes into the film. I knew how she felt. I kept going to sleep and waking up to find they were still quarrelling or dying. I've never been able to watch that film in any language. The only watchable deaths in films are murders.

I was sharing my couch with an Italian sixteen-year-old. He gallantly moved his bag so that I could have one and a half cushions to sleep on. He had two and a half, which seemed a bit unfair as he was shorter than me. After a while, I decided that the most comfortable position was screwed up into a ball with my head on my handbag and my bottom in the air. In the small hours I woke to find the boy trying to turn me into a mattress. He continued snoring loudly and convincingly as he dragged my legs under him and tried to use my bum as a pillow. His friend pulled him off, shouting '*Scende, scende!*' (Get off, get off!) '*Scende la signora.*' The sleeper snored on and got possession of three cushions'-worth of sofa. After that, sleep proved impossible, so I staggered to the loo to try to make myself look human.

There were used sanitary towels horribly in evidence in an open-topped bin. It always amazes me what dirty pigs women can be with each other. Perhaps all lavatories ought to be communal. I'll bet women wouldn't drop those with men around. Beside the bin, the door was marked with '*Monique je t'aime*' and '*Gay è bellissimo*'.

It's nice to know what an influence English has had on the sexual vocabularies of other languages. I'd passed a cinema in Naples the previous day, showing *Erotic Family*. Like the Law Courts opposite, it had a notice saying that it was not for the under-18s.

It was still dark as the ship pulled close to the harbour wall. It had been a remarkably smooth voyage – much more so than any Channel crossing. From reading Homer I'd expected all sorts of trouble – marauding sirens, etc. I've always wondered how

Odysseus took so long to come back from Troy when a Thomson package cruise could do it in a week or two. I'd assumed that the lack of modern technology plus an unusually high incidence of whirlpools and monsters explained the delay. Well, if there were no sirens off Sorrento, then next trip I could dare Scylla and Charybdis. Never trust the word of a married man or a poet.

On the right I could see Monte Pellegrino sharply defined in the clear air. Behind, out on the mole of the harbour, there were clouds of smoke. It looked as if the lighthouse was on fire.

The ferry had docked at 6.10 and it was Sunday. Unless you're an addict of early communions there's little to do at a time like that. I asked one of the sailors where I could catch a bus to the station. All the other people on the boat were being met by cars or coaches. The sailor directed me to a closed customs' gate which proved a problem at first. The rest of his directions were all right though. The streets were clean and empty and already it was remarkably hot. I carried my case in front of me like a baby. I thought it might stretch my arms less. It was uphill all the way, of course. It always is when you're carrying a lot.

Fifty yards up the street a man sprang from behind a parked car, wildly wanking. I stepped round him and carried on to the Via Roma. An old crossing-sweeper told me that all the buses went to the station. When I got in, the only passenger, another old man, winked and told me not to pay. I always take advice like that.

I felt much cooler now, as I'd taken one of my blouses off on the street. I'd been wearing a long-sleeved one under a baggy one. There's a knack to taking your clothes off decently in public. Removing a cardigan is just boring. This is much more of a game – like pulling a tablecloth from under china. You have to undo all the buttons of the undergarments, then pull them out through one sleeve at a time. Sometimes I forget one fastener and all the clothes rise together. Palermo had a good view of my back that day.

I had decided to forgo the unappealing breakfasts on the ferry – cellophane packets of latticework biscuits filled with apricot jam and a tiny black coffee in plastic. Palermo, I had heard, was one of the best places for catering.

Dove Vai?

There was a fly in the bottom of my *cappuccino* in the little bar at the station.

Palermo probably has the nicest first-class waiting room in Italy. My peep through the door impressed me. (I was too honourable to go in.) I always travel second – I can't see the fun of paying extra to travel with a lot of nasty old businessmen and have an antimacassar behind my head.

The bookshops outside sold the usual Italian mixture of trash reading, plus textbooks and poetry. I have to believe that the average Italian is far more literate than the equivalent British person. I couldn't see W. H. Smith selling things like Chaucer in the original to commuters. Yet Dante goes like hot cakes in Italy. There was an intriguing title amongst the educational stuff – *Vademecum del Single Boy.*

I posted my cards in the postbox in the station. Like those outside it had a little sticker USA IL CAP. For a moment I thought that some mischievous Prot had stuck contraceptive ads all round the city in the night. Probably, though, it just means use your boring old postcode. The Italians have one for every city. They are usually made up of the first two letters of the place name, or else the first and last.

I was vaguely tempted to buy some Sibyl Caramels from the bar, as they claimed to have my future written in them, but decided the fly had been enough of an omen.

At half past eight I boarded the slow train to Marsala. It was four hours of little local stops in extremely dirty carriages. The train had come overnight from the north of the mainland and was full of the remains of people's breakfasts, lunches, suppers and breakfasts.

Outside everything looked very clean. There seems to be a peculiar clarity about the air in Sicily that lets you see for a long way. I found I could pick out the individual trees and bushes on hills as the train went by. It was far on in summer. The land looked parched, but the vines and prickly pears were still doing well. Most of the stops along the way seemed to be in the middle of nowhere. At the larger stations a little boy got on and walked the length of the train with a bucket full of iced drinks and a satchel of sandwiches. These boys are a feature of the railway network. They do a sort of nasal howl of all the things they've got on offer: '*Birra, Coke, Fanta, acqua, panini . . .*'

After some salty wastes the train arrived at Marsala, which looked like a one-platform station for a one-horse town. I was wearing black, which is what I usually do for dirty trains. It was stiflingly hot, so I went into the buffet for a sort of lemon-ice drink, a *granita*. This made me feel a lot worse, because the coldness of the ice went straight to my eyeballs. The locals were viewing me with extreme suspicion by now. A soldier came up and asked whose funeral I'd come for. I told him I just liked wearing black, which killed that conversation.

I now had the job of asking if there was a cheap hotel nearby. Nobody wanted to tell me. The barman eventually gestured vaguely across the railway lines and said there was one to the right. I started off, still lugging my suitcase. An old man with one green tooth left in the lower set followed me. He didn't have much hair, just a lot of bristles sprinkled indiscriminately like iron filings over face and head. He told me that I'd never find the hotel on my own, but that he'd help me if I had lunch with him first. I refused this kind offer and darted across the lines, thinking I'd find the place on my own even if it killed me.

I stopped a few people on the road and asked. Eventually a woman told me where to go. Her accent was clearer, so I assumed she'd just been unfortunate enough to marry one of the locals. Her children helped me with my bag and I gave the little boy something as he worked at the hotel. Naturally she'd directed me to the dearer of the two possibles because of this. Still, it was only one night, so I was able to get my value in showers, clothes-washing and toilet-paper.

37

When I'd showered and changed out of my funeral gear, I hit the streets armed with a sixty-year-old guide book which had no map, but detailed all the roads. Unfortunately, most of the street names had changed.

A few turns away from the hotel I was confronted with what must be the most hideous fountain in Italy. It has a bronze sculpture of a kicking donkey, three barrels and a naked woman whose tits spurt. Maybe if I tossed a coin in the water I would never have to come back to Marsala.

Fountain designers are a sadistic breed. They never put a drinking tap or a lavatory near their creations. Yet, invariably, when you hear a fountain, you need to pee or drink, or both.

The *Christian Club Chemise* shop operates near this fountain. It is as dowdy as it sounds and also horribly expensive. The whole town seems very prosperous – probably because of the wine industry. There's an air of eccentricity about the shops – a Persian carpet importer's opposite the station and a café with stuffed sea birds further into town.

By this stage in my walkabout, I had been hailed by several kerb-crawlers saying: *'Dove vai?'* (Where are you going?) They offered me various destinations. It was only afternoon and the full heat of the day, yet already they were making life difficult. In most other towns in Italy they only do this at night. After a while, I realised that absolutely every car was stopping. Every man in Marsala seemed to be a kerb-crawler.

Most of the men in these cars seemed to be in twos. Now and again, one would get out, grab me roughly by the shoulders and start demanding reasons why I wouldn't go with them. *'Perchè no?'* I find it quite extraordinary that any man should want to know why a woman he's never met before doesn't want to get into a car to be fucked by him and his friend a long way from home.

It was Sunday and absolutely nothing was open, not even the churches. All I could do was shake the clutching hands off angrily, cut across roads and double back, trying to get out of the path of each new would-be pick-up. From time to time I answered the *Dove Vai*s with translations of Garbo's famous statement – 'I want to be alone!'

The few men who didn't say *'Dove vai?'* or *'Va passaggio?'* (Going for a ride?) just hissed – a sort of long drawn-out *pss* . . .

Across the town I came on a pedestrian precinct. At least only the hissers could follow me there. On the left I passed the cathedral. According to my guide book this one is dedicated to St Thomas of Canterbury. A ship containing his relics was wrecked off the coast of Marsala and the pious locals took advantage.

At last my guide book was beginning to prove useful. The names of the roads tallied. At the end of Via XI Maggio I could see the Porta Nuova. The buildings here were older and nicer but crumbled by time. On my left there were two museums tucked away through an arch. They looked very thoroughly closed. There was grass in the courtyard between them and the shell of a rusted car. On the left a flight of steps led to the *Pinacoteca*, on the right to the Museo Garibaldi. Just round the corner, a man was advertising electroencephalographs on his side wall. That sounded a lot nastier than Basil Apples of Naples.

I went through the Porta Nuova and turned right into the Giardino Cavalotti. I was glad to get into the shade. The gardens were dark and full of tropical plants and trees. There was a notice by the entrance saying that the area had been officially certified disinfected and pesticided. Nature had left a telling note at the foot of the post – a cast snakeskin. Perhaps its former owner was lurking nearby.

There were large palm trees and oleander bushes everywhere. Near the entrance there was a sinister banyan tree – growing up and down to meet itself. Water bubbled from a metal post almost hidden in the ground at its feet. Behind the vast grey trunk a man was hissing at me.

Everything in that park seemed to hiss. The hot wind crackled in the sun-scorched leaves at the top of the few deciduous trees in the park. It was like sibilant speech. I found myself trying to make out some whispered language. I walked to the end where a dried-up fountain rambled in a series of Baroque steps or levels up to a belvedere. There is a Spanish feel to this part of the architecture. It must have been handsome when the water was flowing. Now the whole thing smells putrid.

I was glad to get back into the fresh air again. The human snake had followed me all round the park. I knew I was near the place where the Sibyl's Grotto is supposed to be. I asked a newspaper seller for the Chiesetta di San Giovanni and was directed to a small chapel in the middle of a piece of waste ground. I passed a larger building on the way – a big impressive Neoclassical 1930s cinema – the Cine Impero. Its splendours were deserted and all the windows had been smashed.

I walked round the chapel and found the doors were shut. There were no notices of services, but the same could be said for a lot of more important churches in Italy. I think the Italians like to make you ask for things. It's probably one of their main entertainments, listening to the horrors of English Italian.

I wondered if I was in the wrong place until I saw the name of the little church carved faintly on one of the doors. The land there is open to the scorching west wind which blows straight from Africa. Every weed is blasted. The dust and the flowers have turned an even grey. I could just about recognise the petrified remains of dog's mercury, fat hen and spearmint in the dark sand at my feet. I saw the same effect in my garden, more than a year later, after the hurricane of October 1987. Then, the only plant that stayed fresh and green and seemed to enjoy it all was my rosemary bush. Perhaps they should plant rosemary in every place where a harsh salt-laden wind blows.

I followed a faint track away from the chapel. I could half imagine I saw the stumps of pillars from a vanished portico, but when I looked closely the stony remains seemed much more like concrete. This path led me to the beginning of the Via della Sirene. The next road to this – the only other romantically-named one in the town – was the Via Sibilla. I walked along this, looking for clues of some kind. I passed block after block of modern flats and a sort of table-football club full of desiccated old men. A starving black cat with one yellow eye ran snarling across my path.

I cut back to the seafront and was harassed by *Dove Vai*s promising ever more distant destinations. One even offered a boat ride. This part of the port doesn't look as if it's changed much since the Romans fought the Carthaginians. I would have liked to walk out on one of the moles and see the town from the sea, but as soon as I started I was followed. It seemed to be the sort of town where you can't be left alone to do anything at any time of day. You'd think the buggers would go to sleep and leave the hot afternoon to mad dogs and Englishwomen.

The shore had the same burning smell as the towns of the

40

Phlegrean Fields. Maybe that sort of air goes with sibylline spots. Either that, or someone had made a bonfire of the weeds. The shoreline was scorched beside the black sand. The water laps close, just a few feet drop down from the main road. Part of the port has large oblong granite blocks like the ones outside Naples. The water is teeming with algae and the greener types of seaweed. It is a clear dark blue though which makes it cleaner-looking than a seaweedy bit of British sea. If it has occupants, at least you ought to be able to see them coming. I fancied swimming, but again couldn't. I felt too much of a target for the passers-by.

I made one more trip out that day, in the evening. As I'd expected, the *Dove Vai*s were even more active. The kerb-crawlers were interspersed with huge lorries full of grapes making for a local market. There was a caramel smell in the air – some vital stage in the local wine-making, I should imagine. By this time I was beginning to have paranoid fantasies. I kept remembering an old horror film I'd seen where the only stranger in town had to be sacrificed to ensure a good vintage in some old French château. I dismissed this idea as ridiculous. After all, in the film, the victim had at least been given a good time first. Besides, most of the local wine industry is run by the English – Ingham, Woodhouse and Whitaker – according to my little red guide book. The English don't do things like that.

Was the town immersed in a sort of harvest riot, I wondered, or were the men always rabid? In the old Dionysian routs it was men who got torn to bits, not women. Mind you, in those days, women stuck together. That September evening I seemed to be the only woman on Marsala's streets. I don't say I blame the others for staying in. On the other hand, I'm inclined to believe women should go out most in places like that, in order to stake an equal claim to the freedom of the road and the night. If men can persuade us that we are only safe when we are with them, that ups their value. Women have to humour them to get small privileges. The most unattractive, vicious man is thus given more worth and more chance of a partner by being seen as a useful protector. Damn the lot of them, I say. I'll force them to accept that a woman can walk alone and doesn't *need* any of them.

I realised after a while that one of the *Dove Vai*s kept coming back. I suppose he hoped that I might think he was the best of a bad lot when I'd turned down a couple of hundred others. I didn't. He was a lout with a clapped-out car, or a clapped-out lout with a car, I hardly remember which. I got seriously annoyed by the way he kept almost running me down, then trapping me in an angle between his car and the wall. I was also infuriated by his persistence in getting out and offering his dubious charms to me. I was so cross that I decided to yell at him the worst possible thing you can say to an Italian male. I was taught this by a carpenter in exchange for similar English expressions during an extremely boring week I once spent on Elba. By now, the fat-thighed lout had followed me to the forecourt of my hotel. I got a few yards ahead and bawled '*Va fa 'n culo!*' at him with a suitable gesture of repudiation. My would-be *inamorato* looked so hurt that I began to find the situation amusing. (Swearing at men is fun – they nearly always get that look – English and Italian alike.) I find it slightly surprising, though, that this particular phrase affronts Italians so much, considering that it only means *go and do it up the arse.* Doing it that way may be illegal in England, but it's something some Italians are supposed to like. The one in front of me muttered a few things that I couldn't quite catch and probably wouldn't have understood. I think he finished with wishing me the same before he went off. I was rather proud of myself. My accent had sounded quite plausible. It's always better when I shout. It's asking for things politely in shops makes me sound very English.

I went upstairs and showered. While I was under the water, the phone rang. I had a sudden fear that the hotel might have given that jerk my room number. Perhaps he had Mafia connections. Maybe he was ringing to tell me he was on his way to do it up my arse. I took a long time answering. When I did it was only room service asking if I needed a drink. I did, but I didn't.

Marsala in the morning seemed a shade more genial. In the hotel foyer I bought a card of the Medusa mosaic pavement which is used almost as a logo on the local tourist brochures. Much as they advertise that pavement, the fact is that it can't be seen, because it lies under the Cine Impero, which has been closed for decades.

A little way down the road I bought a bunch of grapes for my breakfast. They tasted very winy and the black juice ran under my nails. As Marsala is a clean town I only dropped my pips down the gutter gratings. I can't yet face the Italian trick of swallowing them.

The clerk in the Bank of Sicily seemed suspicious of my passport and travellers' cheques. He queried every English word in the passport, then photocopied it all to be on the safe side. I noticed that the bank had the wrong date on the wall – the right day of the week, but the wrong date. That takes talent. Still, at least they didn't throw my money at me like they do in Naples.

I went back to the cathedral and the museums hoping to find something open. The cathedral was, but my enthusiasm for Baroque sculptures, particularly those of Gagini, is limited. I didn't know how I was going to find out about the Sibyl's Grotto. My out-of-date guide said that the key for it was to be obtained from the Biblioteca next door to number 2, Via XI Maggio. Museums and libraries don't usually move, but this one had. There was nothing there now except the *Photo-Jolly* shop. This was filled with pictures of brides. One of them was obviously pregnant. She must have taken a lift from one of the *Dove Vai*s.

It's a pity the men in Marsala seem to be such pricks. Some of the girls there are very pretty and a lot better dressed than the women of Naples. The only thing I can say for Marsalan men is that they are definitely less prone to resting their hands on their cocks than the average Neapolitan.

I tried some of the streets further away from the sea, looking for some other kind of museum with a knowledgeable curator who could help me. There were interesting buildings tucked away here with Moorish touches and funny little unexplained details – a stone cross and wings above a Medieval gate. I popped into the decrepit St Anne's. They were about to hold some important local funeral – probably the one the soldier thought I had come to town for. Outside, beneath a huge cross covered in electric lightbulbs, a fat girl stood waiting with YES in diamanté on her tee-shirt dress. The cross had slipped sideways and a plug and flex dangled, swinging slightly in the breeze.

The man who had sold me grapes boasted that it never rained in Marsala. I wished I could have brought them a good English shower to wash the *Dove Vai*s off the streets. Perhaps Queen Elizabeth should visit – she always seems to bring rain.

I bought a pair of leather and wood sandals for the equivalent of a pound on my way to the station. They were every bit as uncomfortable as what I had on, but at least they hurt in different places.

I was met by a tall gipsy with a baby on the station platform. I thought she was about to beg, but she only wanted to know if I was a stranger and if I was married. When she found I wasn't married, she asked where my parents were. She shook her head in sympathy and disbelief when I said they were in England. I didn't bother to say my father was dead – that would have made me sound even more alone.

As I sat waiting I was joined by a deaf and dumb man. I thought he seemed fairly pleasant – he kept smiling – until he started to go into an awful mime about doing a shit, when he recognised a croney of his. Although he couldn't speak, he could easily manage farting noises. I wasn't going to relinquish my half of the seat, though, just because he was mad. Behind us, I could hear something nasty going on – a murder perhaps – six ticket inspectors were quarrelling in the ticket office.

The train was packed with students, most of whom got out at little stops early on. When I reached Palermo I went straight to the tourist office for a list of cheap hotels. There seemed to be plenty of them. The first few were full up. I climbed flight after flight of stairs with my case and was turned away. I stood on one fourth floor, hopelessly pushing the lift button, only to be told by the proprietor that some fool had left the door open below and that's why it didn't work. That fool was me. At last I found a place down near the docks. The room had blue walls framed in panels and a mock crystal lightshade. The ripples of light were meant to look like the sea. The owner was very proud of this.

I ate out that night. I have been told that Palermo is a very unsafe place, but I didn't find it so. I only had one kerb-crawler after me – you could get that anywhere – and a few *Ciao Bella*s, which are quite good for the ego.

Nuccio

I got down to the docks early to leave my luggage. A Sean Connery clone in white shorts took charge of me and helped me carry my case. In fact he carried it to the quayside and tried to persuade me to hop on a motor boat which was about to leave for a neighbouring island. I could have four days free there, he said, in his *pensione*. He even specified what he'd feed me – swordfish, prawns, squid and lobster – all caught by himself. Taking a lift in a strange boat seems even worse than getting into someone's car. When I wouldn't oblige, he asked the sailors to wait. Presumably he thought he could persuade me, given a little time.

The left luggage office wasn't open. A tiny notice promised that its keeper would return soon. Soon turned out to be an hour. Nuccio said it was his duty as a *moschettière* to wait with me and show me some pictures of the beauties of his island. He also said I must have some breakfast.

Breakfast was a coffee and a *cornetto*. In Italy, *cornetto*s are not the ices that gondoliers snatch from women in adverts. They come in many different forms. This one was a kind of hot cream horn which seemed to be much the sort of state that Nuccio was in. When I'd had my *colazione* he showed me the first four books of pictures. '*La mia amica di Torino, la mia amica di Tunisia, di Francia, di Spagna . . .*' etc. All his friends were shown eating swordfish, prawns, squid or lobster, or dancing in *Il Piano Bar* – one of two attractions on the island. (The other was the baseball club. There were several pictures of its concrete portals with Nuccio in all his gear.)

The fifth book began with six photos of the best flautist in the world. He had been taken so that his flute was foreshortened and looked like a pipe. This album was finished off with a set of couples French-kissing in *Il Piano Bar*. Nuccio said proudly that he was the island's photo-reporter.

There was a long pause before Nuccio brought out his last book. He told me that all the pictures were natural and normal and not porn. These were his English photos of English girls and one Spanish woman. The Spanish one really shouldn't have taken her clothes off.

All his English friends were nude too. Some were sitting on rocks splashing. Others were taking piggyback rides on his shoulders. He told me very significantly that none of these girls had paid for their holidays. I reckoned they were paying now. Two of the girls were very pretty with good bodies. They were sisters. One of them had brought her husband. He still had his trunks on, so presumably he'd paid.

When the nice, normal, natural photos had been put away, Nuccio asked me what I wanted to see in Palermo. I said the museum and the catacombs, if there was time. He told me he knew Palermo really well and could get me to these quicker than I could find them by myself.

Did I like music, he asked, once my luggage was safely stowed. If so, he would take me first to the collection of rare instruments in the conservatory.

The fact that I liked music proved we were twin souls, he told me. I worked for myself writing poetry. He worked for himself repairing motor boats and running his *pensione*. That also proved we were twin souls. He believed in Fate. We were obviously meant to meet.

I soon realised that Nuccio had absolutely no sense of direction. We went around ten blocks with him stopping to ask the way at every turn. At last we found the music school. The one-armed concierge gestured upstairs with her mobile stump and told us we would have to get a pass from the Director if we wanted to see the collection. We went up a few flights with Nuccio lecturing me on plaques, posters, busts and portraits. This composer was local, that one met his girlfriend in a church just down the road. He kept asking me if I knew Bellini, Wagner, and so on.

The Director's office on the top floor was closed. Halfway

down the stairs, Nuccio saw an Art Nouveau poster mentioning Mascagni. *'Conosce Mascagni?'* he asked. I didn't. He didn't know him either, so he started stopping all the passing students for a sort of on-the-spot question-time. No, none of them knew him, either. Soon it was hinted that we should leave.

I was taken to see the Palazzo Mirto next. This palace is not on the official itinerary. You have to visit it eighteenth-century style, asking the servants to take you around while the *Principesco* and *Principessa* are away. It's pretty-pretty, full of small painted ceilings and masses of china. I found myself getting more and more embarrassed as Nuccio picked petty arguments with the footman over whether various pieces came from Saxony or Germany. The servant was glowering with anger. I was wondering if there was anything I could say to defuse the situation. Eventually things relaxed when Nuccio pulled out his camera and got the man to take a photo of *us* in front of some piece of Chinoiserie for his collection.

Our next stop was the Giardino Garibaldi. Nuccio was firmly convinced that I must be a Garibaldi-freak, as I had just been to Marsala. He could not conceive of any other reason for going there. The park had locked gates. They never bother to open them, because vandals have pulled some of the railings out and everybody climbs through the gaps instead. This seems like a sensible solution. The vandals have also written Garibaldi's name in blue paint on his statue. Nuccio was deeply shocked that I wasn't shocked by this. I told him that there was just as much vandalism in England. (They wouldn't have written just his name here.) Italians are so self-pitying about the things that are wrong with their country that I like to tell them we have it as bad if not worse. What have they got to complain about? They don't spend much on heating. Our kids have to buy their own glue to sniff, while theirs can get nice jobs in a shoe factory.

On our way to the museum we went in yet more circles. At least I was getting to see a lot of backstreet life. There was a young girl with a baby in one of the doorways. Nuccio stopped and asked her if she had a husband, was the baby hers and how old she was. *'No. Si. Tredici.'* (No. Yes. 13.) He showed great concern and took a photo of her with the baby. He insisted that the baby's face was to show in the picture, so she had to hold her child in front of her with its shawl pulled back. It was as if he were taking some kind of incriminating mug-shot of them both. Surprisingly, the baby slept through it all blissfully. Then Nuccio posed the girl with her enormous mother. Afterwards he took their names and address, with a pen and a paper which I had to supply, so that he could send copies. I felt like someone who'd been press-ganged into being Dr Barnardo's assistant.

As he walked away he started to lay down the law about how bad it is for any woman to have more than two kids. For once in my life I felt like putting the opposite view. I felt like saying that my singing teacher has seven good-looking, talented children and is happy about that and still looks slim and attractive. Of course, the real reason why Nuccio disapproves of all this fertility is that he can't father children himself. He admitted that later in the day, when he proposed.

We eventually made it to the Museo Nazionale. I only saw the art gallery part upstairs, as I was being bossed around. A lot of the paintings there are Sicilian primitives. They are mostly of a very high standard. But as they were painted on wood they are in poor condition, frayed at the edges, woodwormed, and flaking in places. Most of the artists' names were completely new to me, except Antonello da Messina. I would have liked to make a few notes, but I can't do that when there's anyone with me.

All the pictures are religious. The only nudes are in the Garden of Eden. Nuccio took on himself the mammoth task of reading the labels and telling me the Bible story behind every one. He quite obviously thought I was an idiot. A lot of men think that – presumably because I don't wear glasses.

Nuccio poked all the figures in the pictures as he told me who they were, 'La Vergine, Bambino Gèsu, San Giovanni . . .' He used the tip of his sunglasses for this and scraped them down the saints concerned as he explained about stigmata, miracles, etc. I was tempted to tell him that my great aunt had had stigmata, but I thought it might be too much for him. He had adopted a kind of pidgin Italian for my benefit, with actions thrown in. I've seen similar things done to foreigners in England. I'll always remember the look on the Chinese waiter's face when some old trout told him to tell the chef that the 'Memsahib' was very pleased with the sweet and sour. All that, and she was only in for the £2 business

48

special with her luncheon vouchers. It's not quite so funny when you're on the receiving end.

I'd already had to put up with a lot on the street. Nuccio showed me how to lay an egg, assuming that the look of horrified incomprehension on my face meant that I didn't understand the word 'Uovo'. He also barred me from using a lavatory beside a restaurant, reeling around dramatically, holding his nose. It was great for waiters, he said, but not good enough for me.

He took my photo again in front of a Madonna, because he adored me as he adored the Madonna. I had to blow a kiss at him while I stood in front of, but not obliterating, her.

As I watched him scrape his sunglasses down the blood on Christ's side in a Deposition, I began to understand why the pictures were in that state. Probably a lot of the Faithful had done the same. At this stage I decided it was my artistic duty to lead him up the garden path.

There is a small triptych in the museum attributed to Mabuse. How a Flemish painting got there, I don't know. Nuccio complained greatly because only one side of the painting had been labelled, although there were paintings on both. He obviously thought we'd been had. I was deeply impressed by his version of the Adam and Eve story. Roughly translated it went like this: 'Adam and Eve lived in Paradise making love all day because making love is not a sin.' He kept repeating that bit. 'Then they stole the apple and that was the first sin. So you see stealing is a sin, but making love is not a sin.'

When we'd done all the pictures, he asked what church I belonged to. I told him I was an atheist. It's not exactly true but is a sight easier to explain than having a penchant for the pagan gods. I was sure I had the Italian word right for atheist, but he just didn't want to understand. Eventually, I said that I used to go to the Church of England, but wasn't religious now. He understood that, but didn't believe I could like religious pictures. I explained that I had studied at an art school, but he was obviously still hoping to find himself with a closet religious maniac.

By now, Nuccio had whispered in my ear that I was a siren and he wanted to marry me. He also threatened to come to England for a trip, laden with conch shells. I was tempted to get rid of him at this stage, but, remembering those poor afflicted paintings, I decided to string him along a little further and take lunch off him. Every time we passed a shop with wedding dresses or an advert for bridal mags, he nudged me meaningfully.

On the way to lunch he showed me the best place in Palermo for getting robbed and the best church for gay prostitution. I was also taken to admire the post office built by Mussolini. I suppose he must have done it brick by brick. As one might expect of dictator-design it was very big and drably Neoclassical.

We ended up in a restaurant in Via Cavour. There seems to be a Via Cavour in every town. I can't remember who Cavour is, any more than I can remember what the historical dates that various other roads are named after represent. I'm sure, once upon a time, some pick-up told me, but boring things get blurred in my mind. I suppose visitors to Britain are equally puzzled by our ubiquitous Churchill Ways.

I fancied eating something simple like fish and a salad, but Fate in the shape of a bossy man was against me. I stuck on water because I didn't want to be too legless to get away. Besides, Nuccio had told me that he didn't like his women to take drugs, drink or smoke. He drank and smoked, of course.

Nuccio decided to spoon or fork feed me most of my food and half of his. I had to try the local swordfish, which was very much like salmon, only white. I skipped the *antipasto*, but had to have some of his spaghetti spooned into me. I also had to have some of his mussels, which came in a tomatoey soup. There was a slight accident with this – Nuccio got it all over his flies. I was reminded of a certain scene in *Midnight Cowboy*. His remedy was to stand up and pour a glass of water slowly down the front of his white shorts, while rubbing at the stain with one of the restaurant's pink linen napkins. I drank glass after glass of mineral water to give my lips something to do other than laugh. In fact, I got through two litres practically single-handed, with three trips to the loo.

The waiter came to Nuccio's aid at last with a carton of highly perfumed talc which he sprinkled on the stain. I think it was Lily of the Valley. Some long strips of grilled aubergine were ordered for me. I like garlic in reasonable quantities, but these were covered in great lumps of it – several whole cloves cut into halves. I was spoon fed some of this and ordered to breathe on Nuccio. I usually oblige men in ridiculous kinks because I enjoy laughing at them afterwards. He kept saying he loved the smell of garlic and liked women with good appetites.

Next I had to move on to an extremely substantial ice cream. The waiter was handed the camera to take our photos eating it. Strawberry ice cream has to be about the worst possible thing to mix with garlic. I began to wonder if I was going to hang on to the contents of my stomach.

While I was pondering, Nuccio got us two fiery *sambuccas*. These taste like 100 per cent proof. Evidently, though, they didn't count as drink – women were allowed to have them. We had to link arms – another for the album perhaps – but he kept getting it wrong. I narrowly escaped having it thrown all over me like Joan Collins in the adverts.

When I thought the meal was at an end, the waiter came in with a pile of fruit that Nuccio had bought earlier in a street market. He had washed the figs and stripped and chilled the prickly pears. I was glad I'd refused the mid-morning chocolates, as it just about enabled me to get through the four prickly pears and the few figs he fed me.

A street away Nuccio suggested that we go to a hotel he knew where '*La Signora – Madame – è understanding.*' Madame, *under-standing, Miss* and *donk* (for donkey) comprised the whole of Nuccio's English. He had told me he knew a little when we first met on the docks. It's interesting to speculate what scenario could have provided him with precisely those four words.

I told him that I wanted to walk in the sun. It was the only thing I could think of and put into Italian. It was about as true as when I told the old male chambermaid in Naples that I liked cold showers, a few days later. Still, walking in the sun had to be preferable to going in to see his *understanding Madame.*

Nuccio then got the idea for a trip somewhere outside Palermo. I turned down a swim and settled for the basilica at Monreale. He swore that he could get me there and back in an hour. To be on the safe side I lied, bringing forward the time I had to collect my luggage and be on the ferry by about two hours.

We caught a bus by the station. Nuccio showed amazement that it took more than half an hour to climb a few miles. He last went there as a child, he explained.

Monreale proved well worth the visit. I memorised all the turns from the bus to the cathedral, as I did not want to have to rely on his sense of direction later. The cathedral is what the Italian guides describe as Norman. Italian Norman is infinitely more splendid than English Norman. The ceilings and upper parts were all covered in mosaic and rich with gold leaf. Everything seemed to be in a perfect state of preservation.

There's a vast head and shoulders of Christ the Omnipotent in the apse. (This struck me as strange theologically. Surely it's the Father who's omnipotent?) The inscription is in Greek – perhaps to key in with the Byzantine style. Christ is in the most brilliant of blues and has wonderful six-winged cherubim to the left and the right. I used to try to draw these impossible creatures from Ezekiel's descriptions of them to alleviate Scripture lessons at school. I don't think I've seen any representations of them elsewhere – they're too much of a challenge for 2-D. I reckon they need a hologram to do them justice.

There are thousands of faces of character tucked away on facets of the walls high up – evangelists, saints and Biblical figures. Seeing my interest, Nuccio put 50 lire into a machine to illuminate the ceiling above the aisle. *Sancta simplicitas* – as they said of the old woman who put a faggot on the burning pile beneath a martyr. The light did not go on.

On the street outside we bought postcards. I got several of the rotting mummies from the catacombs I hadn't seen and also one with a splendid bloomer – *Fuga della Madonna*, translated as 'The *Fight* of the Virgin Mary'. Nuccio settled for a picture of the droopiest-titted Eve in the business, with a very long snake beside her. She looked as if she had suckled at least ten kids before she got round to taking the apple. It all goes to show what walking round with no clothes on in a hot climate does for the figure. I looked down at my high ones and felt very superior. While I'm on the subject of Eve, I shall mention something that not a lot of people know. If you read the Bible carefully, you will find that it was only Adam that got kicked out of the Garden of Eden. Another point – Adam called her Eve because she was the mother of all living, *before* they had Cain and Abel.

Nuccio managed to lose the next bus by taking photos of me by the fountain. Eventually we got back to Palermo, which was jammed with traffic. Luckily I was still in time for the boat, thanks to my ruse. I was given a horribly blurred photograph of one of the paintings in the Palazzo Mirto as a memento. It had '*Un caro ricordo di Nuccio*' in very loopy pompous writing on the back. He didn't seem very used to writing, as he took an exceptionally long time to manage this phrase and also to give me three telephone numbers – his *pensione*'s, that of his motor boat business and the baseball club's. I was to ring one of these so that he could send me an air ticket to Palermo as soon as I was free. I told him that I was not on the phone and that none of my friends were on the phone and that I was going to be away touring Britain for months doing poetry readings. (No such luck!) He seemed to believe it all – a religious bloke would, wouldn't he? I gave him a friend's address to send the pictures to.

He had to catch a boat to his island in about two minutes. Before leaving he whispered another proposal in my ear, and also made me promise to wave to the lighthouse on his island as I passed it in the night. He asked me to write a poem about him too. I don't think he'd have done that if he'd known what kind I write.

When Nuccio had gone back to his volcanic home I settled down to another ice cream – my third in twenty-four hours and definitely a mistake. I felt it was my duty to keep eating them, as Palermo is supposed to have the best ones in the world.

At last it was time to catch my ferry. You have to be on board about an hour and a half before sailing. Italians practise a very effective method of queue-jumping. They say '*Permesso*' politely and you let them by, only to find that they've stopped one ahead of you. It's important to be near the front of the line if you don't have a cabin. It means you can get a large area of sofa to yourself in front of the TV. This time I'd let too many people *permesso* me, so I ended up in a tub chair. It was very uncomfortable, but at least nobody could use me as a sleeping-bag.

A little boy carried a beautiful white kitten in a wicker cage up the gangplank ahead of me. Photogenic cats like that get a better deal than the ginger, striped, streaked and patched ones you meet in alleys.

From Naples to Palermo at the weekend, the boat had had a much more cosmopolitan feel. The other direction, all the passengers seemed to be Sicilian. I figured them for farming stock. *Gunfight at the* OK *Corral* was playing on telly. All the vendettas

53

sounded more convincing dubbed into Italian. The men around me were playing cards and talking loudly. My fat neighbour jabbed one of them in the back and told him she didn't want to hear about cars, she wanted to watch the film. I was steadily and messily getting through a small carrier-bag of figs – the remains of Nuccio's market purchases. The afternoon sun had reduced them to a kind of luke-warm, sweet, bruised pulp, but they tasted too good to waste. I realised that I must have looked disgusting eating them, but I reckoned that none of these people would ever see me again.

The telly went on the blink about halfway through the film at a moment of high tension. A fat peasant got up to fix it. He looked more like a pig than anyone I had seen, I thought, until I looked at his son and wife. But who was I to talk after pushing about a pound of squashed figs into my mouth from a paper bag? The pig turned the TV knob round about 180 degrees at a time, causing huge blasts of interference. His wife laughed a lot. In fact she laughed all night. The man obviously figured that he might hit a station sooner or later, before the knob came off. A worried clerk type shushed him out of the way. He managed to get another channel, but there was nothing on it that anybody wanted. The pig pushed him aside laughing and started his act again. He looked so happy playing with it that everybody else started laughing too. It was really much better entertainment than the OK Corral.

I had a few fits of sleep in various horrible positions. The choice was between putting my feet on the sharp rim of the metal table in front of me, or rolling myself into a very small ball within the chair. I gave up in the early hours and brushed my teeth to get ready for Naples. I didn't weaken and wave to any lighthouses. Instead I wrote my postcards. One of these ran:

Dear Lucinda,
    You'll probably kill me for this, but I've given your address to this rather awful Sicilian who wants to send me some photos. He took pics of me with a stray cat in a music school and blowing kisses in front of a Madonna because he adored me as he adored her. I told him I toured Britain non-stop doing Poetry readings and that I didn't have a telephone. (If he believes that he'll believe anything.)
    I didn't feel mean enough to give him a totally wrong address as he'd offered me his heart, half his pensione and motor boat business and a 3-month tour of Italy, Yugoslavia, Denmark, etc.

You're very welcome to open the c/o letter and look before sending it on. I'll write him one telling him I'm about to marry to cool him off then! I bet the photos'll be funny as I was v. soiled and sweaty.

Of course the pictures never came. Nuccio wasn't quite as much of a fool as I thought. Lucinda took her revenge by sending me a postcard from Germany saying that she'd given our address to a member of the Hitler Youth who would drop by and talk about the old days with my mother. I kept telling Mum that it was only Lucinda's idea of a good joke, but she was practically shitting herself at the thought of having to brush up her rusty German. 'I did too much Medieval stuff in the university,' she said. 'It's rather spoiled me for speaking it.'

Cuma

And you may in part easily learn the right religion from the ancient Sibyl, who by some kind of potent inspiration teaches you, through her oracular predictions, truths which seem to be much akin to the teaching of the prophets. She, they say, was of Babylonian extraction, being the daughter of Berosus, who wrote the Chaldean History; and when she had crossed over (how I know not) into the region of Campania, she there uttered her oracular sayings in a city called Cumae, 6 miles from Baiae, where the hot springs of Campania are found.
(Justin Martyr, *To the Greeks*, Chapter XXXVII, translated by Rev. M. Dods, M.A., 1868)

The sun was an impossible-looking dull red disc by the blue of Vesuvius as I walked off the ship.

Naples's docks remind me of a seedy run-down film studio. I don't know why somebody doesn't take part of them for that. They ramble on for a mile or so, with dozens of large deserted buildings, tram tracks and dusty wide streets. The sea and the ships are hidden behind office blocks – a few touches and it could be a desert town or almost anything. There are probably loads of people panting to be extras locally too. You could pick a thousand gladiators or bandits off the streets with no trouble.

I was glad to get an early start. I dumped my case at the station and headed for Cuma. My previous attempts to go there had proved abortive. People in Naples don't seem to know exactly where the Cave of the Sibyl is, or, if they do know, they're not willing to tell. The stop on the funicular railway has been axed, and opinions differed as to whether I should get off at Baia or Fusaro.

At this attempt I opted for a bus to Fusaro. When I got off there was no signpost and absolutely nothing of interest. In desperation I asked a woman with two toddlers. She hadn't heard of the sibyl, but she did know there were some excavations locally. She even told me where to buy the ticket – the local delicatessen – where to catch the bus and how long it would be.

The bus took me to a turning point in the road. The excavations were half a mile further along a quiet lane with ditches full of spearmint and fennel. Like Baia, this was another archaeological park. You pay at the entrance, then meander up the hill.

The Sibyl's Cave – the *dromos* – is at the bottom. It's a coffin-shaped gallery with sharp angles – the walls slope into a narrower roof. It's about 150 yards long, cut into the tufa. Sometimes it's described as the oldest bit of Greek architecture left in mainland Italy. Nowadays, you can walk along it by the natural light which filters in through side passages or cells. At one time these were closed off with wood. The main corridor ends in a little room with a curved arch – the *oikos*, or House of the Sibyl. Before you get to this there are three cisterns in minor arms of the tunnel. These are supposed to be her bath. Christian tombs were cut into this area in the days after the cult died. I don't know why this section is called the *dromos* traditionally. I've seen no explanation for it. The word in Greek means a race, fleeing, running, a racecourse, a length of a course. I can only think that this passage might have figured in a complicated initiation ceremony.

A book on the modern site calls this part soulless as a railway tunnel. Before the archaeologists moved in it was supposed to have had more character. There is one early description of the site as it existed after the cult had disappeared or gone underground, in the works attributed to Justin Martyr:

And being in that city, we saw also a certain place, in which we were shown a very large basilica cut out of one stone; a vast affair, and worthy of all admiration. And they who had heard it from their fathers as part of their country's tradition told us that it was here she used to publish her oracles. And in the middle of the basilica they showed us three receptacles cut out of one stone, in which, when filled with water, they said that she washed, and having put on her robe again, retires into the inmost chamber of the basilica which is still part of the one stone; and sitting in the middle of the chamber on a high rostrum and throne, thus proclaims her oracles.

It doesn't sound all that much like what I was seeing, but maybe in those days, there was an impressive building above the tunnel. Something worthy of the term *basilica*.

On Marvellous Things Heard, which is attributed to Aristotle, mentions an underground chamber at Cuma. Even in the third century BC, when that work was written, the cult of the sibyl was spoken of as a thing of the past.

On the other side from the *dromos*, there are openings and galleries below ground level, where part of the hill has slipped away. Obviously there was once an important complex here. The architecture though is Roman, not Greek. It looks much like the brickwork in the baths and temples of this area. There is supposed to be a tunnel 180 metres long running from east to west, right through the hill of Cuma, but this is not open to the public.

On the path beside there were two headless statues lying at the foot of a rock. Presumably these had once been emperors, as the necks were concave. In troubled, changeable times, sculptors made a standard toga-ed body into which the appropriate portrait bust could be fitted. More exhibitionist emperors had nude bodies, usually those of gods, beneath their faces.

When the hill was overrun by the Goths and later by various brigands, the statues from the higher parts were thrown down. Archaeologists have pieced together many of these fragments for museums. A whole Diomedes was made up in this way. I'd hazard a guess that the headless emperors had just toppled over, as they were not badly damaged. Probably they once stood by the gate.

There are no Italian labels in Cuma. The sibylline parts are marked with various appropriate verses of Virgil in the original carved on modern marble slabs. According to tradition, it was here that Aeneas first rendezvoused with Deiphobe the sibyl. (*Deiphobe* means foe-scarer, so may perhaps be an epithet rather than her real name.) She was the Priestess of Apollo and Trivia. Trivia was the goddess of the meeting of three ways – an infernal aspect of Diana. There are a lot of places where three ways meet on the hill of Cuma. It's an odd idea giving importance to such places. I've always seen more to a crossroads than a slanting T-junction.

The details of Book VI of the Aeneid marry up well with the surrounding countryside. I am tempted to think that Virgil was describing a real ceremony practised in this area. His sibyl acts like a classic medium taken over by a spirit, speaking with another voice. Perhaps she was part of a system of initiation dependent on priestly trickery to make the enquirer believe he'd been to hell and back again. I would suspect something similar went on in the Middle Ages in Ireland, judging by the old accounts of St Patrick's Purgatory.

You climb the hill by the Via Sacra – an old road made of tightly-packed hexagonal blocks of blackish stone. On either side there are bay trees. About halfway up, you come on the remnants of the Temple of Apollo, said to have been built by Daedalus after Icarus's wings had melted. What's above ground – stumps of pillars – looks Augustan. Probably the older foundations are visible from the cliffside. Christian graves have been cut into the old floor.

At the top of the hill – a long climb – there are the remains of Jupiter's temple. The Christians have struck again, changing its orientation, turning it into a basilica with a baptismal well slightly larger than a jacuzzi at the centre. I went down into this and inspected the cracked marble. There was a man nearby, meditating like a Stylite on a stump of pillar, sitting perfectly still and staring out to sea.

The view from here is spectacular – miles and miles of vineyards and shrubs and the sea beyond. There are many ruins hidden and still unexcavated on the private farming land in this area. The hill is well wooded. The top where I was standing had a thicket of young oaks and hazel trees – all far too young to be part of any sacred grove. I thought they might have come from the acorns of acorns of one of the original trees, and took some sprigs as a souvenir. These woods have been frequently cut down in past ages. The hill has on many occasions proved a good hiding place for rebels and brigands.

At the moment it was covered with snogging or copulating couples – all except the top, that is. Every guide had found his prey. It was a pity, I could have done with somebody to show me around. As it was, I found myself having to hurry by discreetly as various girls were being had on tombs or ledges. I could sense their annoyance that this Englishwoman had to come to see the sights.

I was stuck with walking as I couldn't buy a bus ticket near the gates. The bar had sold the last one to someone else. I was told it was two or three kilometres to Avernus. Aeneas had done it, so why shouldn't I? Unfortunately, since his day they've built roads – hot busy ones with squashed cats on the verges. That squashed cat was the only fat one I'd seen in that part of Italy.

A mile uphill into the sun I came on stalls selling whole roasted chickens and fruit. The melons looked good, but I had no knife. I settled for apples and thought I'd try *uve fragole* – strawberry-flavoured grapes. These tasted wonderful at first, but soon began to cloy, leaving my hands stained and sticky. Near the bottom of the newspaper full of them I came on a maggot crawling out of one of the last. I vowed to stick to *muscate* – the large, green, beautifully fragrant grapes. These are perfect in Italy but lose their scent and become ordinary by the time they reach our greengrocers. My apples were banana-flavoured – *mele banane*. It's a bit of a Sodom and Gomorrah area near Naples, with its sulphur-tinged air and strange cross-bred fruit. Even the bees are bent.

Eventually I came to my first sight of a lake, or rather two, way beneath me. The only near-pedestrian was a man on a tractor, but he didn't know which was which. There was a wrecked-looking restaurant built roughly in the shape of a boat beside the road, a path ran down beside it, fenced off with wire and *Vietato Ingresso* notices. The main road ran downhill to the sea. I was back to civilisation, and better still, a station.

Halfway down the line, there was the usual mad rush off the train and I was lost again. I asked the way of two friends or brothers with round faces like ugly moons. They took it as a personal compliment.

My Date

I booked into the same sordid hotel in Naples as before, then went to phone the museum curator from the station. There was a long queue of married men on their way home from work, cooking up various excuses. The phones were simple, illustrated for the benefit of idiots of all nationalities. I had a handful of change and all seemed set fair.

When Antonio picked up the phone he sounded decidedly less enthusiastic. I rather got the feeling he couldn't remember who the hell I was. I told him I was at the station phoning, mainly because I couldn't think what else I could put into Italian easily. He said he'd be there in thirty minutes – at least I *thought* that was what he said. I had just about enough time to pop back to the hotel and change into something a bit more special – a see-through embroidered muslin shirt with a coral necklace. I made it back to the station in time and finished my make-up in public.

By then, I was attracting a lot of attention and being asked if I was waiting for a friend or looking for a man. Had I missed Antonio on the wrong side of the station, I wondered naively. The time was getting on and I was looking very obviously stood up. Worse still, the two friends I'd met earlier with faces like full moons arrived and tried to insist I went with them for a pizza if whoever I was waiting for didn't turn up.

Even if one or other of these men had been attractive, I wouldn't have fancied that. I've tried the double date before. You never get left with the one you want. There's usually some furtive whispered conversation and the good-looking one slopes off, leaving you bought, sold and paid for to his ugly mate. I think there's a sort of unwritten agreement between men on this.

I went back to the hotel and changed into something less conspicuous. I told myself I'd go and have something nice to eat. I was kidding myself though. In my heart of hearts I knew I intended to find someone else. I always seem to make that mistake when I've been stood up. One of these days I'll be old enough and wise enough to curl up with a good book instead. Good books don't let you down like men do.

I started to consider my options like a couple picking a restaurant. 'Shall we go Chinese tonight, or do you fancy an Indian?' I definitely didn't fancy another lying Italian. I hoped I might find a tourist of some other nationality and be able to have a good time with him by taking the piss out of the locals.

My first non-Italian offer came from James, an American, a plastic-jewellery stall-holder. He said he loved me and asked me to come back to his ghetto. He was too honest for his own good. I'm a bit of a stickler for comfort in sex. I've ended up in some ghettoes in my time, but if forewarned I usually say no.

I settled for French in the end. Jean-Claude was about ten years younger than me and had bovine, gladiatorial good looks – masses of curly fair hair – a contrast to all the Italians I'd had on offer. We communicated in Italian with the odd word of French thrown in. I felt slightly superior because his Italian was even worse than mine. Mine is fastish with bad grammar, his was slow with bad grammar.

After a snack I got the scenic tour of Naples by car. He played English, or rather, American pop loudly to please me. I told him I liked opera, but on went more Madonna. I still couldn't see the beauties of Naples even though I was driven to various high points to survey the lights along the way. I admired it all dutifully. I don't really understand why people like rows of lights along roads. My Gran thought the 'fairy lights' that Swansea City Council had stuck up on a tree on the seafront at Mumbles were the most beautiful thing around. I thought so too – at five. By six, I had my doubts.

Jean-Claude kissed me at every traffic lights, keeping one eye on the road to see when they turned green. When he didn't need his right hand to change gears, it was between my legs. He had already started to criticise me. Sex takes a lot of men that way. Why was

I wearing tights? Why was I wearing gloves? The women of Naples didn't wear tights and gloves, he told me. I asked him why he wasn't out with a Naples woman. I didn't really need an answer. The women of Naples may be fat, balding and badly-dressed, but they're obviously not suckers enough to take up with a French bastard.

Jean-Claude then went into a different question and answer routine. I once did a crash course on teaching English to foreign students. I was told that the secret of keeping a lesson going was to ask the sort of questions that couldn't only be answered by a yes or no. Students could just pretend with the other type. They had a 50 per cent chance of getting it right.

Neapolitan men, however, like to ask a series of questions to which you're meant to answer yes. Jean-Claude, living and working there, had fitted himself into this mould. They often start with, *'Ti piace, Napoli?'* (Do you like Naples?) I don't have the heart to tell them that I think it's horrible and filthy – worse than my kitchen on a bad day. I just oblige with a *'Si.'* The Berlitz phrase book from which I learnt my first bits of Italian is all acquiescence in the 'Making Friends' section. It's nothing but, *'Great, I'd love to come!'* *'Thank you, I've had a wonderful evening,'* and *'I've enjoyed myself tremendously!'* None of these phrases were to prove useful that night. By now, Jean-Claude had turned off the road and into some little park. He'd had his hand off the gears long enough to get me fairly turned on. He unzipped his jeans and let the prisoner out. *'Ti piace?'* he said, then, *'È lungo o piccolo?'* (Is it long or short?) *'Lungo,'* I replied. It certainly was, too. In fact, it was so big that I was beginning to have serious doubts about whether we were made for each other, biologically speaking. *'Preferisci lungo o piccolo?'* he went on. I told him I preferred long, because it was what he wanted to hear. He looked very smug.

I had the tights he so disapproved of off by now. The night air was warm and there was a clean wall to lean against outside the car. That idiotic conversation had slightly damped my ardour, but a few kisses put me back on form. One millimetre from entry, he said he thought he heard someone coming. It certainly wasn't me.

I was hustled back to the car for more of the stop-start routine. Three more stops in fact. Each time he imagined observers. I was getting progressively more and more detached. The trouble was,

63

though, that I have some naively honourable ideas about not leading men on for nothing. Besides, I didn't know where I was by now, and he was in the driver's seat.

The final stop was by some iron gates. I thought it might be another park, but everything was so dark I couldn't tell. I could have done with some fairy lights. It was much chillier outside now. I left my skirt in the car, because it was about the last clean garment I had. I didn't know quite what I'd be lying on in that pitch blackness. Jean-Claude had got something from the boot. It was a sort of thin packing material cut in the shape of the car seats. I supposed that he brought it out regularly for these occasions. It was not much thicker than cartridge paper and not as long as either of us.

When I lay down I realised that I was on top of a pile of granite chippings — the sort of thing they put on graves in municipal cemeteries. I hadn't asked him what he did for a living. Maybe he was a grave-digger. Maybe this was his place of work — a spot he used for the equivalent of an office screw. Maybe he was just using me to spread the gravel and finish off his last job nicely. A weight of gladiatorial muscle descended on me before I had time to object. I managed to hit my head on a spade or something that was sticking out. My screams of agony at being trapped between all that unsupported muscle and 40,000 sharp-edged chips were mistaken for cries of ecstasy. He had that who's-a-clever-boy look on his face as he went back to the car to get something for a pillow. This time I got up quickly and suggested that he be underneath. I knew Jean-Claude would be too thick-skinned to come to grief.

Superman managed to come all over me, which seemed quite against the laws of gravity in that position. Still, you can't expect a spoonful from a cock that looks like a yard of ale. Back inside the car, I realised that I couldn't find my skirt. Jean-Claude gestured back to the middle of our love-nest and turned the headlights on so that I could find the little screwed-up ball of material. All the small change had fallen out of the pockets. I slapped the dust off my skirt ostentatiously before I put it back on. Jean-Claude was happily indifferent to this and the scowl on my face. He was busy making plans aloud for the next day. He asked would I like to go to a hotel with him now. Couldn't he have thought of that first? As it was, I felt that he was the last bloke I'd ever want to be fucked by again. I was offered various drinks, but all I wanted was to get back to my hotel and wash the man right out of my hair, my tee-shirt, my bra, my tights and most of all my skirt.

Jean-Claude polished off the conversation by asking me how many times I'd been pregnant. I suppose he thought he'd holed in one.

When I'd climbed to the second floor of my hotel, the old man was on duty. He seemed even more unwilling than usual to give me the tap for the shower. He told me the water would be cold and that I should wait till the morning. I told him I loved cold showers, so he gave in. Then, I found it was occupied. I waited with my bedroom door slightly ajar, ready to grab the tap the minute whoever it was came out.

It turned out to be a man I'd christened *The Stud* because he liked walking round the place wearing only a tiny orange loin-cloth. He had other ideas than giving me the tap. When he'd finished showering, he rushed through my open door, kissed me and said: '*Dove facciamo amore? Qua o nella mia stanza?*' (Where shall we make love? Here, or in my room?) I kicked myself for having looked at him with momentary lust earlier that day. You can't help looking at a naked man in a hotel foyer. I told him wearily that I had a boyfriend and that I'd been with him that evening. (For once bloody Jean-Claude proved useful.) The Stud said I should have two. People greatly overestimate my stamina.

I got my much-needed shower at last and the water was beautifully warm. As soon as I was drifting off in bed, I heard a low insistent knocking at my door. There was a rather sinister cooking smell wafting in from the courtyard, so I wondered sleepily if the place was on fire. I staggered up to put the light on, hit my hip on the metal bed-post, fell over my shoes and struck my head against the wall. The knocking stopped. As soon as I got back to bed, he of the orange loin-cloth — I'd worked out who it was by then — started knocking on the wall from the bathroom next door. After half an hour he gave up and I was allowed to sleep at last.

Men

I set off early next morning, half-expecting that Jean-Claude and car might turn up again.

Ercolano looks like a flourishing modern town. The excavations of Herculaneum are just tucked away in the midst. The ticket man at the gate didn't want to change my 50,000 lire note, so I went to the bar opposite for breakfast. I don't know why Italian banks keep churning out large-denomination notes when almost nobody is willing to change them.

I expected to be cursed in the bar, but as it happened they were quite happy to change my money. The proprietor even insisted I sat down and had a second coffee gratis while he went out to do this. I thought I would come back and buy my postcards there after I'd seen the excavations.

Half the ruins in Herculaneum seemed to be shut, once I started looking round. Most of the houses were barred with little wooden gates about two foot six high. The guides carry keys for these at their belts. I was soon joined by a fat guide who asked my nationality. He wanted to improve his English and asked me to correct him as he showed me round the sights. When I did this, though, he looked offended and soon lapsed to his favoured forms. I talked Italian and he talked English. He showed me a lot of the closed houses. He didn't use his keys – he just told me to climb over the gates. They had to keep all these locked because of vandalism. The houses had dozens of small paintings tucked away. In one or two places visitors had scratched out pictures of vases or carved their names in the middle of the frescoes.

The form of many of these paintings is a small oblong containing a Greek scene at about eye level on the wall. The edges around are decorated with perspectives, or *prospectives* as my guide liked to call them – pillars, steps, sharp angles created by pediments etc. Where these were defective, architectural students have drawn in the parts of the lines that are missing. Some of the walls have an outer decoration of garlands, vases and mythological creatures. The Pompeiian Red in most of these walls was really yellow, I was told, before the gases changed it. Roman painting often has a large area of ground colour. Some of the oldest examples were done on black.

As my guide threw out the dates of various eruptions and earthquakes, the old and the new grew confused in my mind. I didn't know whether he was referring to AD 79 or 1979 until he pointed to some houses on the edge of the excavations and said that the TV aerials on the roofs were all that was left of the ones next door. Apart from that, the place seemed innocent enough, without the burning smell of the Phlegrean Fields. From the main road by the station you could see Vesuvius in the distance.

Herculaneum seemed to me to have a record number of brothels for a small town. I began to wonder if the guide had been taking me in circles. I was shown a casualty of the earthquake – a snapped phallus above a brothel door. He demonstrated what had happened, karate-chopping his index finger. 'Oh my, oh my!' he said in shocked empathy.

Agostino had a snuffly cold, and to up my opinion of him he gave a very macho explanation of how he'd acquired it. His hobby, it seemed, was archaeological diving. While he was twenty feet under, off Capri, his aqualung malfunctioned and he inhaled water. He was lucky to be alive, he said.

There was an interesting swimming race that week, from the mainland to Capri, but he would not be competing. Only the English and Scandinavians were fool enough to do that. (Perhaps he thought I should enter.) He knew, and all the locals knew, that the area was patrolled by a great big shark. This was probably not an old wives' tale, as I remember reading an early Latin passage about fishy delicacies which included blue shark from Cuma.

The fat guide kept telling me I was beautiful – presumably all those semi-castrated phalluses had turned him on. He spoilt the compliment, though, by asking me why all Englishwomen were beautiful. He was exceptionally naive for sixty-odd. He suggested I got England to join with Italy in bumping off Gaddafi. When we'd done him, we could start on the Pope. Well, it was nice to find someone who thought I had influence. Maybe he had mistaken me for Mrs Thatcher — I did have a floppy bow at the throat of my cheap old nylon blouse.

After this I got the tour of the new excavations. This involved being helped over more gates and walked through brambles. I was even given a crowbar to pick at some lava with. There was little to see there but a headless statue and a long building with a stack of broken amphorae and a few empty pedestals at one end.

I'd realised Agostino was after something or other by now, of course. He had made the standard romantic gesture of handing me a bit of oleander. He spoilt this, as he spoilt the compliment, by warning me that it was a) poisonous, b) harmful to the skin, and c) injurious to the eyes. Did I like Italian men, he asked. I said sometimes and turned the tables by asking if he liked Italian women. 'No,' he said, 'because an Italian woman is *come una balena*' (like a whale). He looked a bit like a whale himself.

When we were level with the dusty pedestals the fat guide asked if he could kiss my foot. I've never met a foot-fetishist before. I'd always assumed they went for delicate size-3 specimens in the daintiest of high heels, not size-6 blistered tourist feet. I hesitated in amazement. '*Un momento,*' he said, and lifted me up bodily on to a pedestal. Oh well, he'd asked for it, I thought, and let him have it all dusty from a red-hot espadrille. He proved to have a vast ogre's mouth capable of swallowing at least half of my foot at a time. He seemed to be enjoying himself immensely, muttering '*Che bello!*' or '*Gioia!*' between sucks for the next ten minutes. I kept wondering in a bored sort of way how many other English girls had been shown the new excavations. Soon he started moving his vast mouth up my leg, muttering things about wanting to eat me all up. I didn't want to meet Jonah's fate, so I got off my pedestal. We left the excavations in silence and he passed me on to another guide, saying he must go for lunch as he was hungry. He went off with a sulky '*Ciao.*'

I'd seen almost everything by now — the brothels, the paintings, the vandalism. The whale's best boob of the day was over his description of the parts of a boat. I didn't know the words in

Italian. He didn't know them in English, so he started to scratch a drawing of a ship on one of the walls. I tut-tutted and shook my finger at him, which is the same in any language. He settled for telling me that part of this boat was white spruce and the rest *nuts*. Of course I left that mistake uncorrected. It was going to give pleasure to English tourists for years.

I went back to the bar when I left the excavations, to buy postcards. One of my feet was beautifully clean. The kindly proprietor offered me more coffee, various foods, sweets, even a hotel room and a bath. Italian men must be remarkably generous. I'd only been in Italy a week or two, and already I'd been offered several holidays and many free hotel rooms, not to mention pizzas. This man took the sneaky line – not the familiar *'Dove vai?'* but *'Non ha paura!'* (Don't be afraid!) I find that a particularly suspicious phrase. Why on earth should I be afraid, unless he had something unusually nasty lined up?

My next archaeological trip was Pompeii. By comparison to Herculaneum it was full of Americans and English. There was an obnoxious woman ahead of me in the queue, laying down the law in loud American about how everywhere but here gave her pensioner's discounts. I was so sick of the sound of her that I didn't bother to point out the little notice that said that the Italian government was allowing all over-sixty-five-year-olds in free that year.

Pompeii seems geared to the English-speaking. There were lots of guides talking in it and the stalls were doing a really hard sell. There was a party of Northerners saying they'd never seen any place like it in tones of great surprise.

It was fiendishly hot, much hotter than anywhere else I'd been to in Italy. I suppose it must be the way the sun strikes down on the stone roads. There's not a lot of vegetation. Curiously, though, a few of the houses are used as allotments. There was a well-kept vine in one and hay being harvested or weeds burnt in others.

I wandered through the streets. The ancient baths were open and full of US Marines, sitting lumpishly round the ledges. Some of the most interesting houses were closed for restoration.

The theatre still seems to be used for plays and operas. Some rows of modern seating were being slotted into place. I was more interested in looking for fragments of ancient painting – an enthusiasm of mine. By now I was being hassled by a nasty little guide. *'Dove vai?'* he said, and pinched my arm viciously. I hurried off to look for the house I most wanted to see – the Villa of the Mysteries. It's a more recent part of the excavations. You won't find it included in any of the excellent Victorian books on Pompeii. You have to go along the Road of the Tombs and out through a gate to get to it. The guard there stamps your ticket *Via delle Tombe*.

Inside this well-preserved villa there are some of the largest classical paintings you'll ever see. They are quite unlike the small panels and delicate perspectives of Herculaneum. These take up whole walls with an image. The backgrounds are a jewel-like crimson. The cards which are sold outside ascribe strange, sinister titles to the paintings – *The Domina, The Terrified Woman, The Unveiling of the Mystic Vannus* (a winnowing-fan). They are supposed to illustrate a sequence of the rituals of the Eleusinian Mysteries, but nobody seems to have quite worked it all out yet. There are some small scenes tucked away in large pictures. It's hard to see these at first – especially as several of the rooms can't be entered and must be viewed through windows or from the door. One of the guides was coming out with all his best tourist jokes. 'This is Maradona!' he said, pointing at a satyr with one leg poised.

In the little office at the gate where the guard stamped my ticket, I met a fat man who offered to show me a few tombs on my way back. He looked the spitting image of Falstaff in *The Merry Wives of Windsor* and was about to get as lucky.

Falstaff, real name Matteo, told me he was a chemist from Bologna. (All the older men I've seen from Bologna are horrendously fat. I have heard that the food there is exceptionally good.) His hobby was archaeology. Every year, he came for two weeks to help the students who worked there. I was to help him with his English and he would help me with my Italian. He told me what his month's course in English had cost, then lapsed into Italian. He had a wife and three kids in Bologna, he admitted. I almost began to trust him after that.

Before the tour he patted his belly lovingly and told me that the Signora in his *pensione* in Sorrento fed him too much spaghetti. It's amazing what two weeks can do.

Matteo had a key to the first villa at the end of the Road of the

Tombs. This was once the house of Arrius Diomedes. It had obviously been a luxury home in its day, built next to the sea, before the sea moved out. There were small fragments of *trompe l'oeil* painting. Matteo knew a lot about these and insisted on getting me to view each little piece from exactly the right angle. He positioned me manually so that I could see the perspectives work. At first he did this by touching my shoulders, apologising profusely for the fact that Italians like to use their hands in conversation. Then, one of his hands would slip a bit, or I'd feel his erection pressed into my back. He kept assuring me that he didn't want to make love as he had a family in Bologna and I had a friend in England. He was only putting his hands on me out of friendship. After this, he handed me an exceedingly battered oleander blossom which had obviously seen better days. I have been handed enough tatty free flowers by repulsive romantics to make a barrel of compost. I suppose I was meant to press this one in a book or something, but it went in the bin by the gate.

After the villa, I was shown some tombs and given a few bits of pumice from one. I kept these, but when I got home my mother threw them out, thinking I'd been hoarding cubes of stale bread. A tomb or two further on, Matteo was putting his hands on my breasts or clasping me round the thighs — all in friendship, of course. It's funny how much customs differ from country to country. He asked me if I liked it. I said no. He then asked several times if I liked it a little bit. He was very hurt to find I didn't even like it *'un po'.'* He then said he had to go and eat, warning me on no account to try the cafeteria there. I was probably responsible for a large bout of compulsive eating. It's funny how I drive men to that. The worst case I can remember was that of the sixteen-year-old I picked up a few years back. He felt moved to cook and eat a large steak all by himself after we'd had sex. I suppose I should be thankful he didn't ask me to cook it.

On my way out I stocked up on cards, yet again. The stall-holder insisted I sit down and eat some grapes, then went on to offer me two weeks in Sorrento with him. He was short and bandy with the most virulent, or rather purulent, cold sores I've ever seen. Some days you can only pull that kind of man.

After that it was back to Naples on the *Circumvesuviana* line.

71

Below the main Naples station, the same flattened escalator was moving and piped opera coming over.

For the afternoon, I took the *Metropolitana* to Pozzuoli. Everything there was closed in the glaring heat. I wandered down to the dockside. The older parts of the city were shut off and ruinous. I just looked through the doors of the amphitheatre, which was closed. I wasn't all that sorry. In my opinion amphitheatres are the least interesting form of excavation. I've never liked running. I didn't realise until my mid-twenties that you are meant to kick your legs out behind you instead of raising your knees in front.

There were some good-smelling restaurants near the port, with fish being grilled outside in the square. Soon after I'd passed these a man started following me. He was blond and dressed in bright red, everything matching – shirt, trousers, shoes – and, obviously, stark staring mad. He sang *'Dove vai?'* in a sort of cracked howl. He really pelted it out, swinging his arms about in all directions. Occasionally he did a sort of Cossack leap and clicked his heels to one side about a yard up in mid-air. I found myself walking faster and faster until I broke into a run at the corner. It was not a good idea, as I came to grief on a fish one of the locals had dropped. This was evidently just what my pursuer wanted, as he howled with laughter and went off happily singing and laughing to himself. I wondered as I picked myself up if he had known about the fish at the bottom of the hill. Maybe he even put one there regularly before picking on some poor tourist to chase.

Back in Naples, I finished the day by getting robbed. I'd been warned about muggings and living in bad streets, but when it came the robbery was different. I was in the posh area – near the San Carlo Opera House, and I was on a crowded bus, not walking too near a motorcyclist. The bus was so packed that there were hands on me from all sides. The man behind was stroking my bum, and the one in front had his leg and one hand between my legs. I made the mistake of trying to remove one of these hands. I'll never know which of these two men robbed me – maybe they were a team. They both got off just a stop or two down the road. Just after they'd gone, I noticed my bag was open. I knew it was the sort of bag that didn't do that accidentally, so I assumed that the purse must be gone. Well, at least the thief left me my make-up and my Lucky Pixie.

As I'd just lost about £25 I determined to spend the weekend on grapes to make up – the poor person's answer to a health farm, and no hardship when the grapes are good.

That was the last bus ride I took in Naples. I felt less vulnerable out on the street. To crown it all, after I found my purse had gone, some small peasant attempted to bugger me. He'd got my skirt lifted, and was working up and down, or rather to and fro. He hadn't taken my tights down, though, I'll say that for him. Maybe tights are the only form of contraception known in those parts. Perhaps that's why Jean-Claude had been so annoyed at my wearing them. I trod hard on the peasant's foot – at least I hope it was his – it's a bit hard to tell in a crowded bus.

By the station, a man stopped me. *'Tedesco? Inglese?'* 'Inglese.' 'You give blood? Blood for the little children? Very good!' 'No!' I knew I was a cad to say no. 'Little children' seemed like blackmail, though. I bet if I'd let him have a pint, he'd have given it to some fat local politician instead. Naples had had the use of my body and my wallet, it was certainly not going to get my blood as well. The earlier *'Sangue, sangue,'* was explained. It's a terrible terrible town for tourists.

Underground

I read such things in Homer when I was a Boy; nay, saw myself the Sybil of Cuma hanging in a Glass Bottle: And when the Boys asked her, 'Sybil, what wouldst thou?' She answered, 'I would Die.'

    (The *Satyricon* of Petronius, translated by William Burnaby, 1694)

I became slightly paranoid for the rest of my time in Naples, and carried my money split between small paper bags in a carrier and a small purse under my dress. I don't have the sort of figure that facilitates carrying money beneath my clothes. My mother had suggested a roll of money between my tits, but I had said that this would look like a third tit on me, as well as not being the safest place in Italy. (Between the buttocks would of course be even less safe.) I also drew the line at what 'Cousin Elizabeth', a very distant relative from Penicuik, did. She forced my mother to make her a flesh-pink drill liberty bodice with at least forty pockets hidden away in its vast girth, so that she could go youth hostelling and on pottery courses in complete safety. She had a pattern for it, saved from an old Scottish women's magazine.

I compromised by wearing a small evening bag slotted on to a belt under a side-opening skirt or dress. It looked a bit as if I had a nappy with a pacemaker in it, and people probably thought I was into public masturbation every time I groped for it.

Naples on foot is even more distasteful than Naples by bus. There is an old saying that the place is 'a paradise inhabited by devils'. Personally, I can't see the paradise bit.

It's odd that the place should be so awful. All year round there's a stream of tourists' money pouring into the locals' pockets, yet

74

everything seems deadly poor. Rome, the North, Sicily all look prosperous now, but Naples is falling to bits. Half the churches are closed for restoration, but you can't see much going on. The other half look badly in need of it. Almost everyone is badly-dressed. A lot of the old women are going bald and hobble round in torn, dusty black. Everyone has bad feet. The chiropodists thrive, at any rate. The streets are full of rubbish. The fish-sellers drop samples all over the gutters. The fruiterers throw down their rotten stuff. The kids play football across it all. Everybody drops the paper off takeaway hunks of pizza, rissoles and pieces of battered and salted fried aubergine. There are half-stripped or burnt-out cars parked in the backstreets beneath washing lines full of Y-fronts dripping suds. Starved cats and malevolent pigeons pick through it all. There's no incentive to behave. I found myself adding grape pips by the thousand as I walked along.

There are also some well and truly dirty beggars. The beggars in Rome are more in the gipsy line. Neapolitan ones look as if they've been rolled across an ink pad and odd bits have come clean where they've been dripped on by washing or peed over by one of the muzzled curs that roam the streets.

Some of these beggars sit outside churches and sell little prayer cards of saints with rosy auras and orgasmically rolled-up eyes. Others have little placards with accounts of what's wrong with them. One says he's Austrian and must raise the fare to go back home. He had two incredibly unsavoury sheepdogs with him who sat and scratched and kicked fleas all over him through the day. Every time I passed he looked the same, as if he were glued here, never moving, day in day out, with very little in his box.

The morning after being robbed I thought I'd choose somewhere safe and cheap to go – a catacomb. To get to the main ones – those of San Gennaro (who else?) – you take the road towards Capodimonte. Catacombs are always on the outskirts of cities, so they often get bypassed by the less dedicated tourists. Personally I love catacombs. Apart from containing wonderful art, not too much like a museum – just enough to see properly – they are also good places to get away from the heat. They seem to keep an even temperature all year round. They're good places to avoid getting a tan in.

On the long walk to those of San Gennaro, you cross the Ponte della Sanità — a sort of bridge that passes close to the domes of churches and roofs of buildings on a lower level. This part looked quite interesting. I almost relented in my opinion of Naples. The domes below looked so near you could almost drop things on them — probably all the local *bambini* have tried that, judging by the state of the streets below.

The church of San Gennaro dei Poveri is up a flight of steps. It's big and splendid and in good condition except for worm-eaten mahogany doors. The marble inside really shines. It's not a beautiful church though — too modernised, presumably. Round the back of the outside, well tucked away so that you could miss it, there's the discreet entrance to the catacombs. There are tours on Saturdays and Sundays only, but of course the official tourist maps don't tell you that. Luckily I'd chosen a Saturday. Tours are only at specific times, three quarters of an hour apart. I sat down in the dust and waited and took a suck at my bottle of water. I got covered in ants, but they weren't interested in biting.

The guide was a fat young man in jeans and a red and white bomber jacket. He was bursting out of it all. A few of the Faithful came to join the tour. We waited while he sat in his car, playing tapes of loud Italian pop, with his feet resting on the steering wheel. At five minutes past the tour time he sprang up and took ticket money from us inside the little office. Then, he was off at a run down the steps and into a building below ground level. I nicked a grape or two off a hanging vine and nearly got left behind. He was doing the whole tour at a run. His sloppy look belied his speed. His tongue was faster than his feet. I tried to understand the fastest Neapolitan ever, as he ran ahead over the uneven unlit ground of the passages. He had probably put in his training in a Neapolitan market or bingo hall, if they have such things. I'm fairly used to catacomb vocabulary, so I just listened for the key words like *'mosaico'*, *'affreschi'* (frescoes), saints' names and dates — *'Secolo primo'* (first century) or whatever. These catacombs are infinitely different from those in Rome. The passages are wider and higher. Most of the frescoes and mosaics here are not as high quality and are fairly damaged. They are mostly from the fifth century — later than the examples in Rome. There are heads of St Peter and St Paul, saints offering each other laurel wreaths, etc.

There is one most unusual picture tucked away among the rest.

It shows a Byzantine family — father and mother with a child standing between them. The figures are cut off where the grave space opens in the wall — about three quarters of the way down the parents and halfway down the child. That painting alone is well worth the trip, although the guide hustles you off again before you have time to absorb it. Other works from this period almost always represent saints, biblical figures or emperors and are more usually done in mosaic. This is one on its own. It's a wonderful human record of a time most of us know little about. Naturally, the office above does not do a postcard of it — Peter and Paul, yes, ordinary people, no. Photographic permission is set at an exorbitant rate in all church-owned properties.

The sprinting fast-talking guide got us all moved on. A pious father and daughter in front of me kept asking questions. I was very glad of this, because it slowed him down a little. Then we were out in the sunlight, running across the worn tufa and up the steps again. The guide was living proof that jogging isn't good for the figure. Soon he was back in his car with his feet up, ready to take a good rest before the next tour time was due.

I *could* have gone to the nearby Palazzo di Capodimonte, but didn't. A collection of modern Neapolitan masters and Capodimonte porcelain sounded guaranteed to make me throw up.

I had missed one interesting item in the catacombs, alas. Evidently it has been taken off the modern tour schedule. An old Baedeker describes this as a Medieval hoax — 'a Priapus column with Hebrew description'.

My next venture underground was to be the entrance to Hades by Lake Avernus. I decided to visit this and the Temple of Apollo nearby on Sunday — it seemed appropriate. On my way to the Monte Santo station, I checked with the tourist office to find if the temple was open. The girl told me it was — until one, like everything else.

The ticket office sold me a ticket for Lucrino marked *Torregàveta*. I still hadn't quite sussed out their system. The train was a little less manically driven, out of reverence to the Sabbath. Near Agnano, the part of the coast that has been devoted to thermal establishments from ancient times to the present day, I saw some new graffiti. Someone had chalked out a simple picture of a house on the brown bricks by the side of the line and written CASA

MIAO beside. On the ground, just clear of the rails, there were five assorted tiny kittens – tabby, black and white – staggering round their black and white mother. Two tiny children stood beside, feeding them scraps from crumpled white paper of the sort that the delicatessens wrap round cheese or salami.

At Bagnoli we all scrambled out. My carriage was full of macho men with towels and a transistor on their way to the beach a few stops further on. I didn't miss Lucrino because of the lakes. It's about the only station that doesn't really need a nameplate. Lucrino's lake used to be teeming with life. In Roman days it had a lucrative oyster farm. The sixteenth-century eruption which created Montenuovo cut its size considerably, and, much more recently, a sudden gush of boiling water killed all its fish. It's pathetic and dead-looking now, with a few dry withered reeds near the edge.

Outside the station I came on the Sibilla Hotel, so I knew I must be on the right track. I asked my way to the Temple of Apollo and got directed along an avenue opposite and told to turn left by the lake. The avenue of flat-topped pines went on for about a mile. There were willows and a ditch to the right.

When I got to Lake Avernus I asked the way again of a man I saw fishing there. He said he was from Naples, so he didn't know. That figured.

I walked on round to the left looking for anything remotely resembling a temple. I could see the ruins of some baths on the right, but then I do know my *sinistra* from my *destra*. There was a turning off the lakeside path a hundred yards or so to the left; someone had painted *Grotta della Sibilla* alongside it. I walked up this. After a while it began to look like the sort of byway the police would blame you for getting raped in. The path had little light. The dense underwood had grown up and over it in places. Creepers twined round the bare branches, closing it into a kind of tunnel in places. The earth at my feet was gently curved in the same proportion, so that I began to feel I was walking along a meandering tube. I could now see the cave entrance just ahead of me. There were gaps in the foliage that let a little light in on this. About twenty feet in front I saw an old man sitting with his back to me on an old rusty oil drum. I thought he might be a tramp, as he was tying up a black plastic bag full of things. I wondered if it contained all his possessions. I walked past him to the mouth of the cave. I couldn't see even six inches into the pitch blackness.

I went back to the main lakeside path. Halfway round – less than a mile – there's a restaurant. I thought this would be a good place in which to ask about the temple. The waiter, who was setting out chairs inside, drew me dramatically to window after window in order to obtain the best uninterrupted view of the ruins I'd seen round to the right. They were obviously open permanently, not just till one. They, like some of the buildings in Baia, were of the type known locally as a *truglio* (trough) – a sort of round domed bath or temple, depending on your point of view. Slightly less than half was left of this one.

I turned back and made my way to the sibyl's path again. The waters of the modern Averno looked teeming with fish and weed. There were notices about fishing being forbidden, which had of course proved a great incentive to hundreds of men. The place was alive with them, the way the *Vietato Fumare* carriages are always full of smokers. Italians love breaking rules.

My Baedeker says this lake is 3½ feet above sea level and 210 feet deep, which sounds extremely sinister. It looks a perfect circle in the way that only a volcanic crater can. Guide books describe the water as black, but to my art-school trained eyes it's quite definitely a putrid green. Perhaps from a distance, up one of the nearby hills, it would look black. More probably, people just want it to be black because of the long tradition connecting this area with the Underworld. We are supposed to believe, too, that the lake's name came from the Greek word *aornos* – birdless. Many ancient authors relate stories of how birds could not fly over the poisoned waters. In the book, *On Marvellous Things Heard*, the writer talks of a quantity of swans on the lake.

Averno is otherworldly, but in a different, less crude sense. There *are* birds, and the water's not black, but the light and atmosphere are strange. It reminds me more of the things written of the Celtic Fairyland – the seventeenth-century writer Robert Kirke's *Secret Commonwealth*, what he termed *The Land of the Lychnobious People, The Colonies of the Invisible Plantations* – the world Thomas the Rhymer stumbled into. There's an un-Italian look about this whole area, a marshy half-light and greenness.

There's a lot more truth in old fairy tales than adults would have

79

kids believe. Many of these stories have in fact been lifted out of Medieval chronicles where they were put in as items of truth in the same way that accepted history was. The Lady of the Lake, for instance has a sound basis in fact. She was the founder of a dynasty of doctors – The Physicians of Myddvai – that stretched from the thirteenth century up to the last. Their herbal remedies have been written down. I've tried some of these and found that they work well. Of course, there are a few I wouldn't like to try . . . Thomas the Rhymer, to mention another case, *really* existed. His family, the Learmonts, were prophets for generations after. His works, or some of them, are still extant – a long, prophetic, heraldic sort of poem – one item tucked away and forgotten by most people amongst our wealth of Medieval literature. There are numerous other stories of contact with fairy or other strange people. The Sons of the Dead Woman brought to court to meet William the Conqueror – and many others.

Like various hillocks, burial areas and moors in Britain, the land near Avernus has connections with another race. The Cimmerians, according to the early geographer Strabo and others, lived underground here in clay dwellings, hating the light and only coming out at night. Even now, this area is not as open and sunny as most. They were said to visit each other through tunnels and also to admit strangers to an oracle far beneath the earth. They lived off this and the proceeds from mining plus fixed allowances from the king. They were destroyed by a king who did not like the answer that the oracle gave him. (The more elaborate Castalian fount was similarly destroyed by the Emperor Hadrian much later by being blocked with a huge mass of stone. It had given him the oracle that he would be emperor, and he was afraid that it might do the same to someone else.)

This area was made less sinister in the time of Augustus. The forest was cut down to facilitate the engineering works of Agrippa and his architect Cocceius, a native of the place. This architect cut a tunnel from Avernus to Cuma and also from Baia to Naples. The oracle was removed to another place.

The old man I had seen before was now squatting at the cave entrance. I asked him if the grotto was open and he said that it was, but that I must wait for him to do a few things first. I noticed then that he was filling two little lamps through a funnel with paraffin. The lamps were very rusty. The one he lit had a tiny flame which burnt horizontally in a small jet in the middle of a sort of tin dish. They were definitely not safety lamps. The guide remarked on the dampness there as he went on with his task.

When he was satisfied with his lamps, he put on some extra clothing from the dust bag – a grey-green waterproof jacket, a grey woollen scarf and a strange greenish hat with an eyeshade and ear flaps. It all toned in well with the dim light of the path.

I was told that the tunnel which leads to the Sibyl's Grotto was built centuries B C by the Greeks. It is cut into the tufa. It has been turned black by the soot from more than two thousand years of torches. At one time it stretched two kilometres to Baia. Now, it is only about 200 yards long because of Montenuovo. I have a description of the creation of Montenuovo from Misson's *A New Voyage to Italy*:

In the night, between the nineteenth and twentieth of September, in the year 1538, the earth was brought to bed of a mountain, which has ever since been called the *New Mountain*. Those who have measured it affirm, that its perpendicular height amounts to four hundred fathoms, and its circuit to three thousand paces or a little more. Naturalists have observed several ways, by which mountains are formed; sometimes by earthquakes; sometimes by winds; and sometimes by subterraneous eruptions; as when a mole heaves up earth, and makes those little hillocks which we call mole-hills. It was after this manner that this *Monte Nuovo* was formed, as well as the other new one which I took notice of in the midst of the ancient gulf of Vesuvius. 'Tis said, that there is a pit fifty paces in diameter, on the top of the *Monte Nuovo*; which sufficiently proves that it was produced by eruption: but it never cast out either fire or smoke or occasioned any disorder since those, which were the causes of so prodigious and terrible a birth. The earth quaked; the sea recoiled; the *Lucrin Lake* was almost filled up; churches and houses were set on fire, and swallowed up; great numbers of men and beasts perished; and there was a general and dreadful consternation through all the neighbouring country.

I thought I could see wonderfully well in the dark till I came to this place, the guide's little lamp hardly seemed enough to dispel the gloom. Soon we came to a small opening on the right and he asked if I would like to go down to see the entrance to the infernal regions. Of course I wanted to. This passage was so narrow that we had to go down in single file. The narrowness meant that the light went a good deal further. The path curved downwards. The guide directed the lamp down and warned me that there were small steps there. At the bottom we came to a tiny pool of water from an underground spring or river which disappeared under a low glistening arch. I was told that this was the gate of hell – the river Acheron where Charon ferried his passengers. I knelt down and put my right hand in the pool of cool water. The guide told me that it was always fresh and clean, so I let a few drops from my fingers go into my mouth. The water tasted good. Months later, I learned from a classical dictionary that this river was the favourite tipple of Cerberus and of Tisiphone, one of the furies.

The guide stopped me as I was about to climb the shallow, tiny steps, and removed a very large brown centipede from my skirt. I could see the steps well now, even though his light was behind me. I climbed confidently to the main corridor. A little further on we came to a blocked up wall. It had the kind of diagonal bricking known as *opus reticulatum*. Perhaps this was where the tunnel had been which connected through to Baia in pre-Augustan days.

Turning back we descended another wide passage. At the foot of this were the sibyl's three rooms – square baths with about a foot of water in them. The water seemed slightly bluish in the gloom. The guide splashed a little on the walls to show a remaining trace of Pompeiian Red – the sole remnant of a lost fresco, perhaps. There were also a few scraps of mosaic.

Before we went into these rooms, the guide lit his second lamp from the first, leaving the first behind on the ground. The second one kept emitting little bangs and flaming up all over. He blew it out a few times and eventually managed to adjust it to a small dim jet. After that he led me across two parallel planks that were the only way over the water. Travel books from the last century, or even several decades ago, talk about travellers being carried on the guide's back. Here is an account of C. G. Leland the antiquary's ride:

Just in the middle of the wet, winding cavern, I said:
'You are a good horse.'
'I am particularly good at eating macaroni,' he replied and stopped. This was equivalent to begging.
'Horses who talk need the spur,' I replied, giving him a gentle reminder with my heel. He laughed, and trotted on. However, he got his macaroni.

Of course, a lot of the British are still like that abroad. It's funny when one of them mistakes you for a despised native. This happened to me once in Rome. 'I want to fuck you, Senorita, but I don't want to marry you!' a Liverpool fan shouted to me. I hurried on – he didn't look at all fuckable by my standards.

It was a strange business seeing the sibyl's rooms. I shuffled across the planks until I got to the stone at the beginning of the next room. The third room had to be entered by crawling through a tiny arch in the centre of a block of whitish stone, marble perhaps. The guide put his lamp on top of this block before crawling through. The water in these rooms had tiny little clots – sulphur or leaves covered in sulphur – and felt tepid. This was supposed to be 'The Bath of the Sibyl'. At the side there was a human-length indentation in the solid rock, out of the water. This was 'The Sibyl's Bed'. It can't have been a comfortable life. The tradition of her wish to die is usually connected to her old age. But age happens *very* slowly. *Do* most old people want to die? I think it's only the young, and the very naive young, who believe it's better to die than grow old.

On the right, opposite that extremely uncomfortable bed, I could see, or fancied I could see, some wire protruding from the hole the sibyl was supposed to speak through.

I had gone down to these sights briskly enough, but coming up was a different matter. The way back felt long and difficult. The place was warm and damp. I could feel the sweat pouring off my body. I wondered why the guide thought he needed all those extra clothes. I had a paper hanky pressed to my forehead most of the time, to keep the sweat out of my fringe and eyes. I could have done with one of those headbands bores wear for aerobics. I intended to use the sea nearby to wash off the sweats of hell.

I thought of my guide as a kind of latter-day Cimmerian. He was far too thin, polite and well-spoken to be a Neapolitan. I wondered if this dark, strange man had fantasies about being followed back by Eurydice when he took women down there. I felt I was beginning to frighten him a little. On the way down he kept holding the lamp up to my face to see if I understood what he was saying. Wasn't I frightened of travelling alone, he'd asked. On the long upward slope, as I lagged behind, he turned back to find if I could see.

At the entrance I asked what I owed him, and he said to give what I liked. I gave the same price as at a catacomb. As I left, a party of Germans arrived. I wondered how he'd manage with five of them. Would they all go down the entrance to hell's river one at a time and crawl through the sibyl's stone in file along those planks? Hell is definitely a place for one plus guide, as it was in Homer, Virgil and Dante. Anything else is overcrowded.

Once I'd returned to modern civilisation I went to the free end of the beach — I had nothing worth stealing. There was the same black sand as at Torregàveta and the water had that strange healing perfumed effect. The sand really sticks. I shed a lot of it on the way back to Naples. I was looking somewhat beggarly as I'd left my jewellery off, so I wasn't surprised when a charitable little boy chucked 10 lire at me. (It fits my gas meter well, at home in St Leonards.) I'd already been turned off a church step when I sat down to drink some water. Then, a Neapolitan pigeon crapped on my wrist.

Mary Shelley

I have read a lot about the Sibyl's Cave since my visit. Some archaeologists like to call it a false grotto, preferring to think of it as an abandoned engineering work or a thermal spring for curing some complaint, but they're ignoring the literary evidence as archaeologists always will. It's clear in Virgil that, although Aeneas met the sibyl first at Cuma, a second encounter was arranged for the statutory sacrifices to the dead and the further rituals by Lake Avernus. If it wasn't at the grotto I'd visited, then it was at one very much like it.

Literary tradition connects the land by Lake Avernus with an oracle of the dead from the earliest times. Odysseus was the first literary hero we hear of using it. Aeneas, Hannibal and Scipio all sacrificed here. The clearest account in factual terms is probably that of Scipio's consultation in Silvius Italicus's underrated epic *Punica*. In this case, it was the shade of the sibyl that was raised here by Autonoë, the Priestess of Apollo from Cuma. Scipio's descent and questioning of the spirits involved the sacrifice of a black bull to Pluto, an unmated heifer to Proserpine (she gets a barren cow in Virgil), and sheep to two of the furies – Alecto and Megaera, the one who never smiles. Over these, honey was poured with an offering of wine and milk. Before these sacrifices he had also to dig a trench with his sword and fill it with the blood of black sheep as an offering to the dead. Mercifully, things are simpler now.

Curiously, Virgil hedged his bets – in case he'd given away too many precise details of a mystery religion, perhaps – by making Aeneas return from the dead through the ivory gate of *false* dreams.

In some ways I feel it would be good if they had a woman guide, preferably an ancient venerable one, to the grottoes here and at Cuma. I've only seen a few women guides in art galleries. They are usually about thirty and unspeakably efficient and boring in several languages.

A lot of aspersions have been cast on the interest as well as the authenticity of this grotto. In 1883, Karl Baedeker wrote: 'A visit to the grottoes is on the whole scarcely worth while and should certainly not be attempted by ladies.' Luckily, I'm not a lady, so I found it fascinating. I still marvel as I recollect it and try to piece together the evidence about the sibyl and the cult of the dead.

The sibyl herself is despised by some writers, who see her as a witch – a tatty old woman who couldn't have deserved baths hewn out of solid rock, mosaic and a fresco. If she was the old fool they'd have us believe, it's remarkable that a great empire paid such reverence to her words, that Christian philosophers took her on as an important figure amongst their spectrum of prophets, and that some of her lines have survived and still impress people.

The man who runs the photocopy shop in St Leonards, for instance, has gone to the trouble of studying different manuscripts of her prophecies in the Vatican and Paris. He has also learnt Ancient Egyptian and a few other things for background information. His particular interest is in the part of her sayings relating to Antichrist.

Mary Shelley, after her visit to the Mare Morto at Miseno, the Elysian Fields and the Sibyl's Cavern, wrote in the same vein as most guide books: 'The Bay of Baiae is beautiful, but we are disappointed by the various places we visit.' Years later, however, when both Shelley and Byron were dead, she wrote very differently at the beginning of her best book, that strange, wonderful masterpiece *The Last Man*:

I visited Naples in the year 1818. On the 8th of December of that year, my companion and I crossed the Bay, to visit the antiquities which are scattered on the shores of Baiae. The translucent and shining waters of the calm sea covered fragments of old Roman villas, which were interlaced by sea-weed, and received diamond tints from the chequering of the sun-beams; the blue and pellucid element was such as Galatea might have skimmed in her car of mother of pearl; or Cleopatra, more fitly than the Nile, have chosen as the path of her magic ship. Though it was winter, the atmosphere seemed more appropriate to early spring; and its genial warmth contributed to inspire those sensations of placid delight, which are the portions of every traveller, as he lingers, loath to quit the tranquil bays and radiant promontories of Baiae.

We visited the so called Elysian Fields and Avernus: and wandered through various ruined temples, baths, and classic spots; at length we entered the gloomy cavern of the Cumaean Sibyl. Our *Lazzeroni* bore flaring torches, which shone red, and almost dusky, in the murky subterranean passages, whose darkness thirstily surrounding them, seemed eager to imbibe more and more of the element of light. We passed by a natural archway, leading to a second gallery, and enquired, if we could not enter there also. The guides pointed to the reflection of their torches on the water that paved it, leaving us to form our own conclusion; but adding it was a pity, for it led to the Sibyl's Cave. Our curiosity and enthusiasm were excited by this circumstance, and we insisted upon attempting the passage. As is usually the case in the prosecution of such enterprizes, the difficulties decreased on examination. We found, on each side of the humid pathway, 'dry land for the sole of the foot.' At length we arrived at a large, desert, dark cavern, which the *Lazzeroni* assured us was the Sibyl's Cave. We were sufficiently disappointed – yet we examined it with care, as if its blank, rocky walls could still bear trace of celestial visitant. On one side was a small opening. Whither does this lead? we asked: can we enter here? – *'Questo poi no,'* – said the wild looking savage, who held the torch; 'you can advance but a short distance, and nobody visits it.'

'Nevertheless, I will try it,' said my companion; 'it may lead to the real cavern. Shall I go alone, or will you accompany me?'

I signified my readiness to proceed, but our guides protested against such measure. With great volubility, in their native Neapolitan dialect, with which we were not very familiar, they told us that there were spectres, that the roof would fall in, that it was too narrow to admit us, that there was a deep hole within, filled with water, and we might be drowned. My friend shortened the harangue, by taking the man's torch from him; and we proceeded alone.

The passage, which at first scarcely admitted us, quickly grew narrower and lower; we were almost bent double; yet still we persisted in making our way through it. At length we entered a wider space, and the low roof heightened; but, as we congratulated ourselves on this change, our torch was extinguished by a current of air, and we were left in utter darkness. The guides bring with them materials for renewing the light, but we had none – our only resource was to return as we came. We groped round the widened space to find the entrance, and after a time fancied that we had succeeded. This proved however to be a second passage, which evidently ascended. It terminated like the former; though something approaching to a ray, we could not tell whence, shed a very doubtful twilight in the space. By degrees our eyes grew somewhat accustomed to this dimness and we perceived that there was no direct passage leading us further; but that it was possible to climb one side of the cavern to a low arch at top, which promised a more easy path, from whence we now discovered that this light proceeded. With considerable difficulty we scrambled up, and came to another passage with still more of illumination, and this led to another ascent like the former.

After a succession of these, which our resolution alone permitted us to surmount, we arrived at a wide cavern with an arched dome-like roof. An aperture in the midst let in the light of heaven; but this was overgrown with brambles and underwood, which acted as a veil, obscuring the day, and giving a solemn religious hue to the apartment. It was spacious, and nearly circular, with a raised seat of stone, about the size of a Grecian couch at one end. The only sign that life had been here, was the perfect snow-white skeleton of a goat, which had probably not perceived the opening as it grazed on the hill above, and had fallen headlong. Ages had perhaps elapsed since this catastrophe; and the ruin it had made above, had been repaired by the growth of vegetation during many hundred summers.

The rest of the furniture of the cavern consisted of piles of leaves, fragments of bark, and a white filmy substance, resembling the inner part of the green hood which shelters the grain of the unripe Indian corn. We were fatigued by our struggles to attain this point, and seated ourselves on the rocky couch, while the sounds of tinkling sheep-bells, and shout of the shepherd-boy, reached us from above.

At length my friend, who had taken up some of the leaves strewed about, exclaimed, 'This *is* the Sibyl's cave; these are Sibylline leaves.' On examination, we found that all the leaves, bark, and other substances, were traced with written characters. What appeared to us more astonishing, was that these writings were expressed in various languages: some unknown to my companion, ancient Chaldee, and Egyptian hieroglyphics, old as the Pyramids. Stranger still, some were in modern dialects, English and Italian. We could make out little by the dim light, but they seemed to contain prophecies, detailed relations of events but lately passed; names, now well known, but of modern date; and often exclamations of exultation or woe, of victory or defeat, were traced on their thin scant pages. This was certainly the Sibyl's Cave; not indeed exactly as Virgil describes it; but the whole of this land had been so convulsed by earthquake and volcano, that the change was not wonderful, though the traces of ruin were effaced by time; and we probably owed the preservation of these leaves, to the accident which had closed the mouth of the cavern, and the swift-growing vegetation which had rendered its sole opening impervious to storm. We made a hasty selection of such of the leaves, whose writing one at least of us could understand; and then, laden with our treasure, we bade adieu to the dim hypaethric cavern, and after much difficulty succeeded in rejoining our guides.

During our stay at Naples, we often returned to this cave, sometimes alone, skimming the sunlit sea, and each time added to our store. Since that period, whenever the world's circumstance has not imperiously called me away, or the temper of my mind impeded such study, I have been employed in deciphering these sacred remains. Their meaning, wondrous and eloquent, has often repaid my toil, soothing me in sorrow, and exciting my imagination to daring flights, through the immensity of nature and the mind of man. For awhile my labours were not solitary; but that time is gone; and, with the selected and matchless companion of my toils, their dearest reward is also lost to me ...

Mary Shelley's description is more like the cave at Avernus than that at Cuma. I'd hazard a guess that her initial dismissal of the area was followed by dreams and haunting memories. It would be interesting to know if any of those who have dismissed this place in archaeological or guide books had similar afterthoughts. Probably not – most hack writers do not have receptive minds. Mary Shelley had elements of the prophet in her own character. Her *Frankenstein*, overwritten as it certainly is, has sparked an enormous number of copies, films etc. *The Last Man*, with its terrible plague, could relate to some people's view of what AIDS plus a nuclear holocaust could do to the world. While reading that book, I was reminded of stories of the Yellow Plague that decimated Wales in the Dark Ages, and also of the writings of the Tiburtine Sibyl. These last contain the horriblest, bleakest prediction possible of the end of the human race:

The Antichrist figure will hiss and say: 'Was there a city here ever?' And after these things there will rise up a woman. She will run from the setting to the rising of the sun and not see a man, and she will long for the track of a man and not find it. And, finding a vine and an olive tree, she will say: 'Where is he who planted these?' And embracing these trees, she will give up her spirit, and wolves will eat her.

Waiting

I had just one day left of my first trip. I decided to spend this in Rome on the way back. I thought I would visit another oracle of a kind – the site of the shrine of Aesculapius. This was a male-run affair in its heyday. I'm calling it an oracle because often, where gods of healing were concerned, answers to medical problems were taken from dreams, those of the enquirer or a priest. (For those who wish to study dreams, may I recommend the use of the old traditional method – sleeping in a pigsty. This is supposed to induce prophetic revelations, especially if you share it with a pregnant sow.)

I crossed to the Tiburtine Island by the bridge opposite the Theatre of Marcellus. At this point the Tiber rushes in its way round the rocky foundations. The island is supposed to have been cut to resemble a trireme. The temple itself is situated beneath the Church of San Bartolomeo. The place still has strong Aesculapian connections, as there are several large hospitals nearby. There's a chemist offering acupuncture opposite, and the Israeli hospital next door.

St Bartholomew's is a pretty church. The styles of various centuries from the eleventh on have combined well. It has a Romanesque tower. The only inharmonious element is provided by a set of twentieth-century sculptures in the portico outside the doors. These have obviously been carved by the twee-est of wankers. St Francis, with his long loping arms like a bendy toy, is easily the most nauseous.

Inside, the light is rosy thanks to highish windows, faintly tinted pink. That seems a bit indecorous for a church, but it suits the

Baroque elements quite well. The place was empty and smelt of incense.

I had to ring at the sacristan's door beside the church to be allowed down the crypt. He had an entry phone which I had slight problems with – disembodied Italian without the gestures can be very hard to understand. I kept saying I couldn't hear well. By the time he popped out to take me through the church, he was obviously annoyed at realising he had a deaf English lunatic on his hands.

The crypt isn't all that interesting – the sole item left from the shrine is about eighteen inches of old pillar set into the wall. There are also a couple of eagle and serpent columns from the church's early days, which perhaps tie in. The shrine was set up here when a sacred serpent jumped ship and swam ashore.

I left the church and crossed by the Ponte Cestio, heading towards Trastevere. On my way I passed the Basilica of San Crisogono. Inside, there are columns from the baths of Septimius Severus. Outside, the twentieth century has struck again. One of the Faithful has left a striking offering of pink lilies tucked into a useful little gap between Christ's legs on a crucifix.

I satisfied my thirst nearby at my favourite drinks stall. This sells all sorts of interesting freshly pressed mixtures like lemon juice and coconut milk. Then it was time for the long train journey home.

It was several months before I could make my next trip to Italy. A series of readings at literary festivals and a catastrophic winter full of burst pipes and falling ceilings kept me in England.

I meant to learn more Italian, but didn't. I did however research sibyls diligently and look at charts of the temperatures in Italy, longing for those few degrees more. (I did not realise that those temperatures were only average ones, created in spring by a quickly alternating series of highs and lows.)

I didn't get away till April – the rainy season. My final hold-up came courtesy of the Canadian Broadcasting Corporation. They wanted to interview me, they said, on the way back from doing Anthony Burgess in Monaco. I sat and waited and they never came.

I had a lot to do on my second visit – the places connected with the sibyl in Rome, her temple in Tivoli, some Virgilian remains in Naples, a fountain oracle near Padua, an Etruscan place or two and the closed grotto in Marsala. So much mileage would be involved that I bought a freedom of the rail ticket. This time I would take the train to Sicily, via Scylla and Charybdis.

I was flying out with no passage back because I could only get a cheap flight one way as it was near Easter. I told the travel agents airily that I would get the train back. The clerk promptly refused to sell me insurance. Taking a one-way ticket obviously amounted to suicide in her eyes. (The bank, as ever, was willing to take my money.) They're an odd breed, travel agent's clerks. I'd heard her older workmate tell someone over the phone that there were no women working there, only *Ladies*.

After getting a cheap ticket with difficulty, I found the plane was only half full. A voice thanked us over and over again for flying with them. We'd been transferred from a small aircraft to a British Caledonian last minute. (Mercifully it was raining and the air hostess had the full dazzle of her tartan uniform hidden under a raincoat.) The voice told us that there would be interesting films for us. These turned out to be *Dangermouse* and half an old sit-com.

At Turin there's a view of snowy mountains. There are no Burger Kings or Healthworks as in Gatwick. Security is an armed policeman who mutters '*Dove? Dove?*' (Where? Where?) to a young Alsatian which dutifully licks every suitcase and handbag as we go by. I felt tempted to pat the dog, but thought I might look suspicious. He might even sniff out the condoms in my bag.

I had some hours to spare before the night train to Naples, so I headed for the cathedral, meaning to see The Shroud. Naturally, being Sunday, it wasn't open to visitors. In fact they have slightly odd hours – weekdays from 7 for the Faithful, 9.45 for tourists. The cathedral is not remarkable. It has one enjoyable painting in the Chapel of Saints Crispin and Crispinian – eighteen tables of the lives of these saints round a central Virgin and Child. It's one of those rather primitive sixteenth-century paintings with a lot going on in it. It's by Defendate Ferrari, a painter you don't get to hear about at art school, mainly because half his work is truly awful. There are a lot of paintings by him in the nearby art gallery.

The Palazzo Madama, which seems to be entirely staffed by women, is a highly likeable collection with nothing modernised or didactic. It's full of Piedmontese, Lombard and Alsatian worm-eaten Virgins and French tourists. It also has wonderful pews, chests, carvings and misericords, even a platter with John the Baptist's head on it – cast all in one piece in brass – a collection of vast keys and Vercellese's portraits of the ugliest baby angels ever recorded. As with many of the not-so-well-known galleries in Italy, there are also a few masterpieces tucked away. There's an Antonello da Messina portrait and the strangely humorous picture of a game of chess by Sofonisba Anguissola. I was thrilled to find a first-class painting by a woman. That's something else an art school doesn't tell you about. A tart plays chess while a jester advises her. There are all sorts of undercurrents between the men – knights, scholars, courtiers and the three women. It has eight portraits packed in. There's an air of intrigue like the sub-plot of an Elizabethan play – a sort of cynical *Love's Labour's Lost* feel. The fashions are depicted in minute detail down to the screwed-up green kid gloves in the woman player's hand and the chain that hangs from the marmoset's nose in the fur that trims her cloak. She has captured several pieces and a screw-on top like a crown lies by – presumably to make a queen out of a pawn. Somehow, though. I don't get the feeling that this is serious chess. It's too interesting – much more of a spectator sport.

Upstairs in the palace part of the museum there's the china and glass collection. It's all classified by region and looks very thorough, although I'm not enough of a china-lover to tell. The collection contains everything from a wolf to a cabbage and is mostly life-size. The glass is rather well displayed – against a window – so that you can see the square outside and the light coming through. It's a much better effect than any modern lighting system.

The floors of the palace are what I like to think of as eighteenth-century parquet. They creak horribly. The walls are all carved and papered in silk. There's a wonderful dark room with *trompe l'oeil* of peacocks and exotic birds coming through windows on the ceiling. It has a wooden model of the palace on a table – it's called the Castle of Rivoli there – about ten feet by four in mahogany. The carved statues on the battlements look strangely real. It's odd that paintings of sculptures or statues sometimes do. It's as if the second artifice is homoeopathic.

Outside, everyone was walking off their Sunday lunch and window-shopping. Turin must be about the dearest place in Italy for clothes. The cheapest thing I saw was a designer flasher's mac

— a snip at a few hundred thousand lire. The other shops were filled with extravagantly cut sweeping sable coats. The city is gracious — very de Chirico — huge nineteenth-century squares, some with Gothic touches to the buildings, and long porticoes full of shops. There are lots of mock Medieval bronze heroes on pedestals in the squares and parks, all gone a brilliant verdigris green.

All the people seem to be remarkably well-dressed, in spite of the prices. I was in crumpled corduroy after my long journey. The only other ill-dressed woman around was touting for custom in lemon trousers and a bright lilac ski anorak.

I wanted to be in Naples by the morning, so I had the bright idea of catching a *Rapido* to Genoa, spending an hour or two looking round before the slow late train.

Genoa looked very attractive from the train, but as soon as I was a block or two away from the station, it started to pour. The streets were full of rotting veg and limping, red-eyed, starving cats. Some old women in black were busy feeding these with mortadella and spaghetti outside the church of St John the Evangelist. '*Ha mangiato? Vieni qua, vieni qua.*' (Have you eaten? Come here.) I contributed my airport butter. St John's is the darkest church I've seen. Inside I could see a loon in loon's glasses praying by some tapers. He kept turning and looking as he prayed. There was a whole case full of silver-plated Sacred Hearts, most of which were propped against the thigh of a prostrate dying Jesus. Outside my espadrilles soaked up the pee in the cloisters as I hastened back to the station. I thought about going to the *Sexy Cinema* to waste an hour or two, but, as I hesitated, a prim Milanese offered me half of his umbrella to the station and saved me from a fate worse than getting wet.

The station is like Genoa. It has a grand front, but the inside's a let-down. I got my first taste of waiting-room life here. Unlike British stations, the Italian ones never close. All Italian waiting rooms are filled with alcoholics and lunatics. It's a very compassionate system, the way they're allowed just to live there. In Britain, the poor buggers would be arrested if they didn't have a few pounds in their pocket — the pathetic amount that saves you from being classed as a vagrant, but isn't enough to buy you accommodation or a decent meal in a restaurant.

Some of the inhabitants in this room had reached the stage of *delirium tremens.* There was a mutterer with a hearing-aid, some-one who kept clawing the air near my bottom, a few who howled and yelped and a bag lady or two. One of the bag ladies had a full-size weighty bouquet at her lapel, a huge rosette on her belly and a six-inch brooch on her shoulder. Her friend had a floral skirt down to the ground and kept washing her hands in the air. A few sailors rolled in and a drunk told them I was a *'putana'* (a prostitute). He kept trying to fix up deals with me. I turned my back and he muttered *'Porco Dio!'* Then an addict came in. She struck up a bargain with an old man and they left. One of the old women started to massage her tits – round and round and round – another old man paced up and down watching her. He had a nose like a lamp. I kept wishing I'd gone to the *Sexy Cinema.* I went down to the platform and found a smaller waiting room. I realised now that this was where the normal Italians waited for trains. I'd only tried a second-class waiting room. I wondered what the first-class ones had – grade one psychos, rich heroin addicts?

I thought about taking a train – any train – to get away from the station. All that was on offer, though, was one to La Spezia – where Shelley was drowned. After that shower I felt drowned enough.

The family opposite me on the train to Naples which goes on to Palermo by the late evening had a lot of luggage and a cat box. Every now and again a long brown arm came out through the wicker bars. Eventually they let it out – a chocolate point Siamese kitten. She snuggled down for the night on the mother's lap, purring loudly.

Virgil's Tomb

I had time for breakfast – coffee and a pastry – before taking the *Metropolitana* to Mergellina. Mergellina is the clean end of Naples – the bit Jean-Claude had taken me to for the view and the lights. Virgil's tomb is round the corner behind the church of Santa Maria Piedigrotta. This church is plain by local standards. The holy water receptacle has a line in Latin about purging with hyssop, but there's no hyssop and no water to hand.

The tomb is in an interesting little park with other remains. There's a plan of it all by the gate. The paths slope up steeply. On the way you pass a bust of Virgil. I stood on the edge of the pedestal and kissed it for poetic luck. The tomb itself is like an ancient columbarium. It's about fifty feet high, with steps up and round. It has a flat top. Plants of all kinds grow out of it. (Any vegetation that survives away from, or above the earth – mistletoe, house leek, etc. – is believed to have magic or healing virtues, or to be spirit-haunted. Grass from a statue's head was used to cure headaches.) There are bay laurels at the top. Legend has it that these grow again as often as they're plucked. There are a lot of them on Roman tombs though, so maybe that has nothing to do with this one belonging to a poet, not unless it's mostly poets buried down the Appian Way. There are also brambles, ivy, roses and various herbs – wormwood, thyme and marjoram. I've noticed tombs often sprout marjoram. I once tasted some from Sir Francis Dashwood's in Bucks, above the Hell Fire Caves. I like eating herbs along the way. I take a certain pride in this from my childhood, when I was the only London kid around who knew which fungi and plants were OK. I enjoyed the pig-ignorance of other kids who hadn't learnt any botany and had been told to eat nothing by their parents in case they were poisoned. It was my first taste of the one-upmanship of the outsider.

There's a tiny room at the foot of the tomb, which has been turned into a sordid kitchenette with a very unsavoury sink and a few tools. At the top, there's a square temple room. I went inside and saw a Roman bronze tripod repaired in iron, containing a withered flower arrangement – sprays of bay gone copper-coloured, the odd dead rose and herbs. There are ten niches in the walls. I wanted some of the bays as a souvenir, but thought I'd prefer a fresh bit. I slipped under the railings outside and went to the edge for a leaf.

Near the tomb there's the start of an old aqueduct, with a damaged, once good fresco of a Virgin and Child plus Saint on the rock face beside. There are a lot of unsavoury pigeons nesting in holes in the brickwork.

The site of Virgil's tomb was bought and restored by the poet Silvius Italicus (26–101 AD). It's in quite a good state now, but it isn't listed on the local tourist brochure as something worth seeing. Silvius Italicus was a reasonably good poet in his own right. His *Punica* has more colour and readability than Livy's prose on the Punic Wars. He was so Virgil-obsessed that he kept that poet's birthday (October the 15th) rather than his own. He also had a collection of busts of Virgil.

Silvius Italicus was not the only person to feel like this about Virgil. Martial states that the Ides of October were sacred to him, just as those of August were to Hecate, and those of May to Mercury. The *sortes Vergilianae* were used as a form of fortune-telling. You could enquire into the future, opening a volume at random, or else set up a more elaborate system – choosing several lines, one commenting on another, just as several cards are used in a spread. Other books have been used for this – chiefly Homer, the sibylline works and the Bible. I am particularly fond of bibliomancy myself. I usually use Shakespeare. I find that only really good writers are usable for this. It is a good test for one, in fact. All the best authors produce powerful adages about life that can be used in this way. It often makes one see a new light on their works – applying an odd sentence or line of poetry in a different context. Shakespeare gives very humorous oracles. One day, when I had asked too many similar questions, he lost patience and came up with: 'How now, mad wag?'

Virgil has been one of the biggest influences of all writers on thought and learning. Because he wrote the Fourth Eclogue, which is considered by some to be a prophecy of Christ, his works were found completely acceptable when those of many other pagans had fallen into abeyance. (In monasteries where a rule of silence was observed, books were asked for by a sign – scratching the ear – as pagan writers were thought of as equal in status to dogs.) Because of Virgil's clarity of writing, the *Aeneid* was used for centuries as a grammar book. Many people knew his works by heart. A new, rather unoriginal, poetic form grew out of this familiarity. Writers produced *centos* – verses made by stringing a number of separate lines of Virgil together to make a coherent piece on a particular subject. The knowledge in Virgil's writing is so encyclopedic that he could be made to say almost anything on almost anything.

There are also many curious Virgil legends around. By the Middle Ages he had become a magician. In a way, by writing about the sibyl, he annexed some of her qualities. Many early Christians ranked them both equally as prophets of Christ. They are both characters in miracle plays. In Poland, there is still a game of the *Simon says* variety, using Virgil's name. Our *Simon says* . . . is, of course, based on Simon Magus. (St Augustine put the sibyl in as a citizen of the City of God.)

There is even a legend that St Paul went to seek the bones of Virgil. (He had wanted to find him living, seeing a suitable convert, the story runs.) Instead, he discovered the subterranean chamber where the poet had been buried. Access was difficult, due to a storm, terrible sounds, etc. Eventually the apostle found Virgil, seated between two lighted tapers, with a mass of books thrown about the floor. Above him, a lamp hung. In front was an archer with a drawn bow. At the threshold there were two bronze men wielding steel hammers. St Paul was able to stop these, but when he entered, the archer let fly his arrow, which put out the lamp, and everything fell to dust. The apostle had wanted to bring away some of the books. It's interesting that the Aeneid would have been destroyed if Virgil had had his way. (Our Chaucer, another poet who's good for oracles, as he writes good one-liners, similarly wanted part of his own works destroyed.)

The monkish chronicler, Gervase of Tilbury, relates a different story on Virgil's remains. An English scholar, he says, was offered a gift by Roger of Sicily. He asked for Virgil's bones and went to Naples armed with letters from the King. At that stage, no one knew the position of the grave, so the people were quite willing. By means of his arts, presumably black ones, the scholar found out that they were in the centre of a mountain. The body was uncovered, perfectly preserved, with books of magic (or experimental science) under his head. The Englishman kept the copy of the *Ars Notoria*, but the citizens felt that their city would be unsafe without the remains. The bones were removed to the Castel di Mare and shown, behind iron bars, to visitors who wished to see them. The Englishman said that if he had been allowed to keep these, he would have learnt all Virgil's arts from them by means of a spell which would have taken forty days.

I am interested in what makes a book, or a reputation, survive. The sibyl's fame has lived beyond the burning of her books. Reginald Scot's *Discoverie of Witchcraft* is reprinted and readily available now, in spite of James I's attempts to rid the world of it. (The book is more sympathetic and more sensible in its attitudes to witches than any other from the sixteenth century.) Gervase of Tilbury's works, however, are not easy to get. Unlike those of most of his contemporary chroniclers, they have not been translated, or even printed in their entirety in the original Latin in this country. On the surface, this seems a shame – the bits I've read look interesting. In some ways, though, there's poetic justice in it. Gervase was a bastard of unparalleled proportions. There's a story on record of his betraying to the Church as a heretic a French girl who'd refused to have sex with him. The girl was burnt.

Tradition says that the bones of Virgil rested in what is now known as the Castell' dell' Ovo. Another of the magician stories says that this castle was founded upon a kind of palladium – an egg in a bottle – and when this was upset, Naples would be finished. (Now that sounds like a good idea . . .) For many centuries a sack containing Virgil's bones was shown to visitors. A storm could be produced just by shaking these bones or letting them out into the air. I was to visit this castle later.

The Suetonius biography makes it fairly clear that Virgil was homosexual. Naturally, because of this there was one Christian legend that was anti him. When Christ was born, it said, all the *sodomites* including Virgil died. Well, there've been plenty of them since.

After I'd seen Virgil's tomb, I had just about enough time to buy some fruit and get a bus to the station for the mid-day *Rapido* to Rome. I got some unspeakably juicy *Pagani* oranges, and small withered *annurche* apples. These apples look in a bad way outside, bruised, battered and purplish, but they're perfectly white and good-tasting within. They are supposed to be very good for your health.

The oranges still had bits of hard stalk and leaves attached. This looks very nice, but goes straight through any carrier-bag pretty quickly. I scattered them everywhere as I boarded my bus. That was how I met Antimo. He helped me stuff the oranges into my handbag and tie a knot in what was left of the carrier to keep the apples in. He told me he was a civil servant, but not a civil servant, because he also wrote and painted. I know a lot who think like that in England. He only did the work for money – he was also a student at the university at Fuorigrotta.

There are an immense number of perpetual students in Italy. There are lots of discounts allowed, which probably explains why most of them want to keep a foot in the door educationally. Naples station even offers half-price cups of coffee. Mind you, as they're overpriced in the first place, that doesn't make a lot of difference. I always feel slightly sad that I can't get student discounts. There didn't seem to be as many around when I really was one. My trouble is that I feel about fifteen within. I don't believe in observing the decencies of getting old. My body's in much better shape than it was ten years ago. I want to look as near beautiful as I can manage. I don't want to knock years off my age. There have been and always will be women who're attractive at thirty, forty, fifty, whatever. Women shouldn't have to lie about their ages to comply with the fantasies of men who only chase twenty-four-year-olds.

In fact, it's men who ought to be more insecure about ageing. Baldness is a sight less curable than superfluous hair. Female fat is more sexy than male fat. We could get a large bum and tits – they only get a belly large enough to obscure their cocks. And then there's impotence . . . When you think about all that, men have a lot more to worry about than women. That is probably why they have systematically sought to make us insecure through the centuries.

Antimo was a little younger than me, although a little old for being a student. He was quite good-looking and his finger-nails were about the same size as mine, so I was sure he couldn't be from Naples. I asked, and he said that he came from a tiny village up Mount Vesuvius, which didn't sound very safe.

He wanted me to take a later train, but I didn't really feel like getting involved or, worse still, getting to Rome too late to find accommodation. I told him that I only like travelling by *Rapido* trains. These are fast few-stop trains like our InterCity ones. He helped me aboard with my luggage and we had a goodbye kiss. I knew there was only about two minutes to go, so the affair couldn't last long. Then, there was an announcement . . . The station gods were on his side, as the 12.00 *Rapido* was rescheduled to become the 12.48. Forty-eight minutes is too long for a parting kiss, so the situation in the corridor deteriorated rapidly. How much can you do in a train corridor? Quite a lot, between passers-by. When Antimo was a more relaxed man, he asked my horoscope sign. Scorpios are passionate, he told me, which I knew already. He gave me his phone number. I'd told him that I would be going to Sicily after staying a few days in Rome. He pointed out that Naples was between the two geographically – something I prefer to forget. The phone number just joined all the other ones I've lost in my time.

Rapido trains are very clean and civilised. I was entitled to travel on them with my runabout ticket. Other passengers had paid a supplement in order not to have to mix with the low types who travel by slower trains. They were all very well-dressed and well-behaved as the *Rapido* was on its way to Milan. Milanese tend to be like that. I didn't feel I fitted in. Apart from my activities in the corridor, the oranges were making me a rather unlovely companion. Kissing is thirsty work, so I felt I had to eat five of them when I returned to my place in the tightly-packed compartment. *Pagani* oranges squirt everywhere – they're much juicier than anything obtainable in England. I think they were all glad to be rid of this nasty British tourist by the time the train stopped in the suburbs of Rome.

Roman Women

In Rome I found a *pensione* quickly. I knew from past experience that there are a lot of cheap places in the streets a block or so to the right of the station. The right side of stations always seems the best place in Italy – from a miser's point of view, anyway. Besides, it's not far to carry your luggage.

The first few places I'd passed had *Completo* on their doors. It was getting to Easter so everywhere was filling up. I settled for a double room, rather than look any further. It was as cheap as a single anywhere else, with plenty of hot showers thrown in. The owner was incredibly houseproud. She did nothing but walk round with a spray aerosol of polish and touch up the clean mirrors all day. She even did it while she was booking me in. She didn't seem able to stop, even when she was phoning her husband. She told me she must phone him to see if she could let the double as a single. I think she suspected I was about to entertain a string of lovers. I heard her phoning her husband again later when a non-married American couple arrived asking for a room. The man told her they were friends and just liked to share a room wherever they went. She rang the husband and they were allowed to stay. In the few days I was there I never got to see or hear the great man. I saw the mother-in-law though. She looked at least ninety, was totally deaf, very suspicious and slow on her pins. You could go and take a shower and she'd still be halfway across the hall on your way back.

I wondered about the absent landlord. Did he feel grateful for his wife's deference, or was he off picking up tourists, secure in the knowledge that she'd accept any explanation the *superior* sex gave her. Italians, on the surface, all seem macho. Of course, we'd say the same of the Roman Empire. The truth about that, though, is surprising. Rome was ruled by women's words in its religion – first by those of the nymph Egeria, then the sibyl's.

Egeria was a muse, a *Camena*. One of the early kings of Rome, the Sabine, Numa Pompilius, was admitted to her sacred grove and married her. Under her instruction he caught the gods Picus and Faunus and forced them to teach him how to draw Jupiter from heaven. Jupiter appeared in the form of lightning and promised a public sign of favour. Next day a shield fell from heaven while Numa's citizens were assembled. He had eleven others made to match, so that no one would know the true one, and appointed the twelve *Salii*, the dancing priests of Mars, to look after them. He also created four pontiffs as a sort of ecclesiastical council. For the special service of the guardian gods of Rome, Mars and Quirinus (Romulus), he appointed two *flamens*, and one also for Jupiter. For divinations, he created four *augurs*. He appointed the Vestal Virgins and built a temple to Vesta. The other temples he built were to Janus and Good Faith. He started the yearly festivals of the *Terminalia* (concerned with boundaries) and the *Paganalia*, which had to do with *Pagi* (districts). He was merciful, only allowing the harvest festival type of sacrifices. He divided the people into guilds, according to their trades or professions. He also determined the public holidays and changed the calendar from ten to twelve lunar months. That seems quite a lot for the reign of a king. All his ideas came from a woman.

Numa put aside great treasures for sacrifice to the gods. It's recorded that these were sold in haste in the Mithradatic Wars, under Cornelius Sylla. The price received for a part of these was 9,000 pounds' weight of gold. Interestingly, Sylla's family name is a corruption of *Sibylla*, and came from an ancestor's connection with the interpretation of her works.

Numa also left books of magic, or philosophy, depending on your point of view. The garbled legendary version says that these were dictated by an evil spirit and found by a country man ploughing the land near Numa's tomb. Historians vary the account. Cassius Hemina specifies that the books were found in Numa's coffin and that they were made of paper soaked in citrus oil to prevent moth and placed on top of a square stone tied round with waxed cords. The contents of these books are variously stated as the teachings of Pythagoras, pontifical law, the decrees of Numa, and the antiquities of Man. All versions state that the books were burnt after they'd been found – most say that this was by a decree of the Senate. It's interesting that the original books of the sibyl were also burnt – by accident – during the Sylla crisis.

Little evidence of Egeria remains in Rome. *Parco Egerio* is marked on the map by the old *Porta Capena*, where she and Numa used to meet. Most of this park has been swallowed by a restaurant, an oratory and private gardens. Now, there is only a bank of daisies and a water fountain at which I once filled a water bottle. This water tastes very good at first, but, sad as I am to have to admit this, it goes stale very quickly.

About half a mile outside the gates and the old wall, the Appian Way starts. One of the first tombs there is that described as the Tomb of Romulus. It's a circular building with one or two nice scraps of fresco of charioteers. There are also some sketchy cartoons of emperors. They are actually quite like the Gilbert illustrations to the *Comic History of Rome*. A modern map at the entrance to the tomb marks a spot dedicated to Egeria and a sacred wood. It has greatly distorted the angles of the roads and is too inaccurate to find these by. If it is to be believed at all, these should lie round about the car park of a snack bar past Caecilia Metella's tomb. Maybe the pine trees in this and nearby gardens constitute the sacred grove – but I doubt it. This snack bar advertises *granitas* as its speciality. If you haven't tried a *granita*, don't.

Of the sibyls, there is little more left in Rome. There were once three statues of them, now there are none. The books, which were bought by Tarquin, were kept on the Capitol in the charge of two men, then, later, fifteen. It was their job to consult and interpret – often when there were alarming portents – the statue of Apollo dripping sweat at Cuma, showers of blood or stone, or the birth of a hermaphrodite. Some of the oracles given would indicate that this sibyl favoured a bloodier form of worship than her predecessor Egeria – but maybe that was only the fault of her interpreters. Look what Torquemada made of Christ's words. The college of fifteen priests also kept the *libri fatales* of Veii, the *Carmina Marciana*, the sayings of Begoe the Etruscan prophetess and the lots, or *sortes*, of Albunea of Tibur. In 83 BC, the books were burnt when the Capitol caught fire during the Sylla crisis. Five years after, a commission of inquiry was sent out to collect verses from other parts of Italy and Erythrae. About 1,000 lines were collated. Augustus, and later Tiberius, destroyed various lines from among these as spurious. Again, the words, false or true, were at the mercy of men. Always, the unwanted verses were destroyed with fire, leaving no possibility of their recovery. Augustus transferred what he thought genuine to the Temple of Apollo on the Palatine – the beautiful hill that stretches up from behind the Imperial Forums. At the end of the fourth century, the books were officially burnt. By that stage, most of the power had gone from Rome.

Now all that there is to see on the Capitol relates to the latest of the sibyls – the Tiburtine one. Albunea was alive in Augustus's time, which makes her considerably easier to think about than those lost in the mists of antiquity.

The museums on the Capitol have nothing about sibyls, but there's a wealth of good statues in them – almost too many to see in a day. I sometimes look for resemblances in an idle way. Apart from gods, emperors and portrait busts, the museum on the left has one of the most beautiful mosaics extant – a small delicate one of doves eating from a bowl. While I was admiring the busts, a British tourist asked his American friend: 'How about two of those for your mantelpiece?' 'Oh shit!' the American said in horror.

The Capitol has been used for many things in the past – plays, bull-baiting, even crowning poet laureates. Petrarch was done here. Tasso, unfortunately, didn't live to make it. The next coronation there wasn't until 1725 – that of Bernardino Perfetti. He had a strange childhood – a bit of a smart arse like San Gennaro, some might say. He was reciting the *Ave Maria* at eleven months, did a line of poetry at one and sonnets at seven. History does not say if he took time off to fill his nappies. The third coronation was that of a woman, Corilla, in 1776.

Corilla (real name Maria Madeleine Morelli Fernandez) charmed most by her wit. A great violinist of the day often accompanied her. Sometimes he laid down his instrument in admiration. She was married to a Spanish nobleman whom she dumped.

Hardly anything of hers is known now, but, like Perfetti, she was supposed to have been good at improvising, a talent much appreciated at that time in Italy. She was already famous in Rome, Naples and Florence. Maria Theresa had called her to Innsbruck to celebrate the marriage of Archduke Peter Leopold and Maria Louisa of Bourbon with a poem. Catherine the Great would have liked to have her at court. She presented her with a pension, which her successor, Paul the First, continued to pay. Strangest of all, perhaps, the Pope, Clement XIV, authorised her to own and read the forbidden books.

On her way to the laureateship, she was received into the Arcadian Academy. This had been founded in 1690 to make war on bad taste. (It was probably about as useful as the Royal Academy or the Poetry Society in fighting that.) When she was made a shepherdess she took the name of Corilla Olympica. Before going on to be crowned she had to go through a peculiar set of questionings. She was asked about the colouring matter of the iris by the Pope's doctor and about the loss of eloquence after Cicero's death by an advocate. Then she had to prove that there was no virtue without piety and improvise on the theme 'Pastoral Life'. Next day, in front of an audience of writers, ladies and cavaliers, she was questioned again . . . 'Why did fable give Cupid darts to aim with when he was represented with a band across his eyes? What was the first revealed religion and who revealed it?' She then had to set forth the arguments that a European would have to use when explaining the advantages of a law to a savage. The women asked if men or women generally proved more faithful. Corilla's last test was by twelve members of the Academy. There were questions on the beautiful in art, heroic poetry and the physical and moral proofs of the existence of God. Eleven days later, with the approval of the Pope, Corilla was crowned.

Her coronation was on Saturday August the 31st. (She was nearly fifty at the time.) She was conducted to the Capitol by three countesses. The Pope's Swiss Guard and the Senator's militia were drawn up on the square. She was crowned under a canopy of crimson velvet in the consular hall by the first of the Conservators. He was dressed in a golden robe. The mortars of the Capitol fired a salvo of 100 discharges. Verses were read by Arcadians, and Corilla improvised on the splendours of Rome and the high value set on the laurel crown. She also covered the superiority of modern philosophy and the influence of Christianity on art. It's interesting that poets always have to be right-minded. I wonder if the West would care tuppence for a Russian *non-dissident* writer?

The church of Ara Coeli, which has beautiful Pinturicchios, is supposed to be the site of the sibyl's prophecies relating to Christ. The sixth-century writer John, Patriarch of Antioch, gives this version. To put it briefly: Augustus wanted to know who would succeed him, so he went to the sibyl. At first, she gave no answer. Later, she told him that he must leave because a Jewish child was born who had subjugated the other gods and ordered the temples to be forsaken. Then the Emperor had an altar built on the Capitol with the words *Ara Primogeniti Dei* – Altar of the First-born of God.

The Western version of this tale is a shade more elaborate. Augustus went to the Tiburtine Sibyl to ask if he was a god. She asked for three days to make her divinations. Then she told the Emperor that a king had come to earth in human form to judge the world. The Emperor then saw a vision of a virgin standing on an altar holding a child, and was told that the virgin would conceive the redeemer of the world. The spot where he had this vision is where Ara Coeli now stands.

There are many other legends about the Capitoline Hill at Rome. One of these places a Virgilian work of magic there. This consisted of a house full of images representing the various countries of the world arranged round a statue of Rome. When a nation was about to threaten war or revolt, its image would turn its back or ring a bell, depending on which version of the story you read. Others make this a magic mirror in a tower, a kind of *camera oscura* perhaps – for seeing what occurred at a distance. The house, or tower, was supposed to have collapsed at the birth of Jesus. The same is sometimes said of the temple which preceded the Ara Coeli church. Early Christian and Medieval writers seem to have a great urge to fabricate or quote anything that shows a great chance in the world coinciding with the birth of Christ. I suppose the Roman historian's love of prodigies is carried on in this. Anyone would think that early Christians didn't find the birth important or authentic enough without outward omens. I have a theory that a thoroughly prejudiced old man sat down in his study prior to a well-deserved martyrdom and invented the lot. Like the original gospel that modern theologians believe lies behind three of the present ones, this document is of course lost. We just have a scattering of the lines from it spattered across the pages of Augustine, Salicetus, Lactantius, etc. So what did this old man invent? A voice saying that the god Pan is dead, various temples collapsing, the oracles stopping, Virgil and all the homosexuals dying. It would seem that the world became less rich as it went into its AD phase.

For many years I believed that widespread early Christian fiction about the oracles. Now I know that an impeccable pre-Christian source disproves it. Cicero states that Apollo had stopped making verses by the time of Pyrrhus (third century BC). He hints that the power of the places where prophecies were given had faded with Man's credulity. I think there may be a subtler reason. Cicero also states that the whole song of the sibyl was written in acrostics. The initials of lines showed the prophecy covered. Eunapius writes that the Pythian Oracle invented hexameters. Plutarch tells us that early Delphic prophecies were in verses. As time went on in Delphi, less literate priestesses were employed. The oracles then became prose. The theory behind employing uneducated women was that they couldn't have the intelligence to fake it or half-remember verses from school, instead of being just empty vessels for the God's voice. (After the rape of a young priestess at Delphi, women of fifty dressed as maidens were put into the job. Men like to believe that women of fifty are no temptation. Yet, in practice, women can get raped at any age. It's just another way of frightening and humiliating them.)

To be uneducated and unable to make verses at fifty takes a particular kind of cloddishness. If there is such a thing as inspiration, then you need a good mind to be able to use it. You must be trained, whether that comes from an educational establishment or years of reading on your own. You have to be very smart to be a poet or a prophet. You can see this best perhaps by looking at the character studies of them in the Old Testament. They're people who're unafraid, or else able to face their fears. They can cheek a king if the need arises. They're definitely not arselickers. The religious would say God inspired them. An atheist might say that it was anger at what was wrong with their times. Police Chief Anderton, with his good salary and uniform, has about as much hope of being a prophet as a fart has of staying in a paper bag with a hole in it.

108

I can see a parallel to this cessation of true prophecy in the poetry world — the decline into romanticism. Logic and good grammar are not considered a necessary part of poetry any longer. I used to think it was my bad French when I looked at poems by Symbolists and the sentences seemed to lack any main clauses. 'Muses and gods get blamed for everything,' as I once said in a poem.

Is it that hard to prophesy in the sense of foretelling the future? In most cases you have a 50 per cent chance of getting things right. That's more than the chance of getting a job or having a poem published. If you phrase things ambiguously enough, people might not even know if you fail. A little elementary logic might tell you the outcome of an election — you could top up your record of right predictions by making easy ones like that. Another thing that helps is that there are a lot of occult-loving men and women out there, wanting you to be right, even if you write as obscurely as Nostradamus.

Of course, even if people go out of their way to make things true that doesn't make a person less a prophet. Jules Verne was right about the name of the first rocket to get to the moon, even if the Americans gave him a helping hand. The mission *could* have failed, as a recent rocket-launch did.

I have to admit that the ability to foretell the future exists. There is a vast body of evidence on the subject. The daughter of Caecilia Metella — she of the tomb — is one of many people recorded as having had a prophetic dream. It's always hard to tell the truth of such visions though, unless they're well documented at the time. Some are perhaps just people being wise after the event. Other cases cannot be explained as easily. There is, for instance, Swift's statement in *Gulliver's Travels* about the satellites of the planet Mars, Deimos and Phobos. According to an astronomical book I have at home, he quotes correctly the times they take to orbit, long before this was known to scientists. There's no way that can have been faked. No one could have known that Swift had made a correct prophecy until after his death. Interestingly, there are many such stories connected with writers from the earliest times on. A genius, like a king, attracts legends.

I bought a postcard of the altar that commemorates Augustus's vision, but the actual thing proved impossible to find, although I was told by an old monk that it was near the Temple of Helena. This mini-temple has a truly disgusting modern bronze of the Empress – all streamlined with a very small head. It bears absolutely no resemblance to the ancient statue of her in the Capitoline Museum next door. This shows a rather beautiful woman with an unusually large bosom.

Like the sibyl and Egeria, Helena, the mother of Constantine, was quite an influence on Roman religion. It was she, it is said, who brought the marble stairs in St John Lateran's from the temple in Jerusalem. It is a truly amazing sight, if you go to this church in Rome, to see the people – in the proportion of three men (tame husbands) to about forty women – kneeling their way up these stairs, a prayer to a step, in order to knock a few years (or is it a hundred?) off their purgatory. A step in time saves nine? Every time I've passed these stairs I've had a strong urge to sprint up them. One afternoon, I waited outside the church for opening time, half intending this. I was eating kumquats, which were cheap in Rome. I was sharing the step with two Indian nuns, a strange-looking girl and her mother and sister. The girl pointed to my shoes and said *'Scarpe!'* Then she pointed to the cloudy sky and said: *'Luna! Sole!'* as if she really saw the moon and sun. She started to look through my bag, so I gave her a kumquat. She took one bite into it and froze with a look of horror. I told her it was good and ate one myself to prove all was OK. She then promptly swallowed hers, pips and all, rushed through the door as it opened, and went fast up the stairs, leaving her mother and sister kneeling in shock at the bottom.

Goodbye Flavia

For Tivoli you take the bus from Via Gaeta. It goes the long way round and takes about an hour. There are lots of Americans there. The bus finally stops at a sort of park called the Villa Gregoriana, which contains the Sibyl's Temple and other remains.

Once inside the gate, my eyes became wildly allergic to something – probably a sickly-smelling white-blossomed evergreen tree. The right one streamed with tears and the left just went red. An old man came up and insisted on doing a *Brief Encounter* scene with his hankie, which only made matters worse. Then he suggested I bathe my eyes with water from the fountain, which worked perfectly. After that he elected himself guide to the area. I was taken first to the cascades of the Tiber, which were being photographed by Germans. The old man took a great delight in telling me they hadn't chosen the best view. The best view was from a lower stage.

The whole area is well-wooded and full of good old British weeds like Jack-in-the-Pulpit, brambles and nettles. You need to get your calf muscles in training for Tivoli. The Temple of the Sibyl is visible from most angles on the hill opposite. This means that you go down all the steps on one slope and then up all the others on the side – in theory. In practice it's worse, as there's a multiplicity of deviating paths and flights leading to grottoes and scenic views. My guide was already telling me what not to see. In contrariness I said I'd see everything.

Between the two slopes, the Anio meets the Tiber. The downhill stretches I could take fast and easily. The uphill ones I was forced to take at speed because the old pest refused to take his hand off my bottom. I could feel my heart pounding as I was pushed up flight after flight. I kept hoping he'd be the one to have a heart attack first, as long as I didn't have to give him the kiss of life. I had a long sit down and a drink of water on the bench below the temple, so that I could race up the last flight.

The temple is that of Albunea, the Tiburtine Sibyl. (*Tibur* is the old name for Tivoli.) Albunea's image was found by the falls of the Anio with a book in her hand. These were transferred to the Capitol. It's generally believed that all the sibylline prophecies have been much tampered with by Christians, in order to make things fit. Still, the opening part of her writings shows the kind of respect she was held in. It describes her coming to Rome and being met by the entire city, including the 100 judges, that wanted her to interpret a vision they had had. They started by addressing her: 'The wisdom and understanding of your Majesty are great.' She took them to the Capitoline Hill to give her interpretation. In the version I read it was covered in olive trees, which sounds more like a link with the Mount of Olives than Rome. Still, olives grow well enough in Italy, so it's not impossible.

The temple in Tivoli has ten or eleven pillars intact. It is round, with an inner room which has a block of stone, a window and a door. In some ways it is better viewed from a distance. Close up I was only conscious of its emptiness, the lack of statues, frescoes, mosaics, furnishings, and . . . people.

There is even less left of the Temple of Ceres next door. It has a gutted, desolate look. I went out by the restaurant in whose back yard it lay. My pest of a guide told me the Villa d'Este was the only other good bit of Tivoli, so I went there. I must learn not to take advice from men. It was fountains, fountains everywhere and never a drop to drink.

My one pleasure there came from seeing another painting by a good woman painter, Lavinia Fontana. (The Capitoline Museums include a few paintings by women, but they're fairly run of the mill.) The one in the Villa d'Este is just a simple portrait of a man, a teacher or scholar perhaps, in Martin Lutherish black with a book in his hand. The background's so dark that it almost absorbs the velvet of his clothes. I would like to see something more complicated by this particular artist. Fontana had nine children and a few miscarriages. Luckily, her husband was supportive – you can't really blame him for not using contraception in the sixteenth century – so she was able to travel around executing commissions for altarpieces.

Outside the gardens of the villa, there were yet more steps. My leg muscles were beginning to feel hamstrung and pulled in ways they'd never known before. Going up St Paul's is nothing to Tivoli. I passed a statue that looked the way I was feeling – a lot of the iron was showing from inside, it had green legs, scrunched-up tits and no head.

Everyone was taking photos – husbands took pictures of their wives going behind the water in one long curving fountain. Others, students usually, preferred to be taken next to Diana of the Ephesians – the one with forty tits, a number of which squirt water. Everything in this garden was overdone – the mermaids on one fountain had four screws to each tail. By one wall, the other side of which had a huge drop, there was a notice telling people not to jump.

On my way to the bus for the Villa Adriana I sampled a few streets. There were a lot of pedigree cats and songbirds in cages in evidence. The cages are hung out swinging over the street. Near the bus stop I saw the town's memorial to the locals who had opposed Fascism. Only four names appeared.

The Villa Adriana tries very hard for schools. It even has a Museo Didattico, which is extremely didactic. There's hardly anything in it but plans and photos. Only on the top floor is there any statuary – a few *small* bits. There's an ugly head of a girl, for instance. She's so ugly, in fact, probably no other museum in Italy would give her house room.

Outside in the Roman ruins, all was chaos – several teachers had lost their school parties. Most of the little boys preferred playing football on the grass to seeing the Museo Didattico. One of the teachers was going berserk, but it was obvious who was boss. Away from the baths and the forums and the barracks and the children running races, there was part of a Temple of Venus. A nice statue of her remained, so I offered up a quick prayer and went on my way.

The bus back was stuffed with Americans. They'd all done Tivoli. They were doing Rome in the next two days before they finished off Europe. One of them was Italian-speaking. He was told: 'You can ask Giovanni to get us a cab to the Coliseum, but don't take any bullshit.' The Italian-American got talking to me and found out I was a writer. He told me he'd always remember my name. 'Goodbye Flavia,' he said as he got off the bus.

Ostia Antica

The next day I headed for Ostia Antica. I'd seen almost everything in Rome at least twice in previous years, so now it was the suburbs for me. To get to Ostia you have to take the Metro beneath the main station. The service has got a lot worse in recent years. It used to be straight through and fast. Now there was only a pissy subway left where the train used to start from – it smelt nearly as bad as the Doge's dungeons in Venice.

I changed trains halfway and eventually got to Ostia together with a bunch of German tourists. Ostia is my ideal sort of country-side – ancient flat-topped, sweet-smelling pines, cypresses, ruins and wild flowers everywhere. There are small bee orchids, the flowers of which almost look alive enough to sting in the wet grass, and masses of calvary clover with its blood-spotted leaves. One of the Germans was trying to find a four-leafed clover on an oxalis. She was as much a born loser, I thought, as the drunk who once tried to get his hand up the inside of my tight black satin trousers in a pub.

I was walking along the Via delle Tombe when I met Roberto, one of the guides. He was quite good-looking in a brigandy sort of way. He was being nice to a fat smoky stray, which endeared me to him. I assume, sometimes wrongly, that men who stroke cats gently make better lovers. I believe, from certain hints dropped by my discreet mother, that my father used to stop to stroke the cat while he was doing it.

Going round with a guide is always an assault course – you get helped over walls and down steps. This time I was balancing in the rain with an umbrella, like a tightrope-walker, as I was taken along the alga-ed edges of underground sarcophagi to see the separate places where they laid jewels or ashes had been laid.

Roberto had a kind of water-fixation. He kept taking me down below ground into Roman cisterns and water systems. It was very dark and the rain dripped through the gratings into the mud below.

Back on terra firma again, I was shown the House of Apuleius. It was small and not very opulent, as one might expect of one belonging to a writer. I have loved his *Golden Ass* since I first read it at twelve. I remember quarrelling with my mother because she had kept me from reading it far too long. So what if it's full of sex and bestiality. I gave her a copy of Rabelais illustrated by Doré for her next Mother's Day to give her an idea of the sort of books she should be recommending.

Roberto showed me the plinth where the statue of Cupid and Psyche had stood. He demonstrated with me the pose they had held, but his version was more Rodin than Classical.

I was getting a little wearied and puzzled by our trips beneath the earth. At one point, after saying his usual '*Qui passava acqua . . .*' (Here water ran) Roberto told me he needed to go '*al bagno*'. The bathroom turned out to be the nearest Roman cistern. I turned my back demurely as I heard zip, gush, zip. I felt very English standing with my umbrella.

At last I got the pay-off for my subterranean ramblings. I was taken down an old bath complex, round a corner in the dark, led by the hand, my feet almost leaving my shoes behind in the stickiest of mud. Then, in front of me, I saw a most marvellous statue – a small opening in the ground above let down a shaft of light on the man-size figure of a god astride a bull, pulling back its head. My guide told me it was Mithras.

There are various statues, paintings of initiates, and *Mithraeums* scattered through the Roman Empire, but the religion was too much of a rival to Christianity to be allowed to survive.

The cult of Mithras, the Lord of Light, was all-male and involved a series of painful initiations, so I can't be all that sorry that it went. Nobody knows exactly what was done, but the ordeals seem to have been by water, fire and fasting. The followers were divided into seven grades – Raven, Bridegroom, Soldier, Lion, Persian, Courier of the Sun and Father. Some of the clothes they wore are represented in paintings of the day. The Raven had a head mask, wings and a dark red tunic and carried emblems of Mercury. The Bridegroom wore yellow with red bands and sometimes carried a lamp under a veil. The Soldier carried weapons and was in white or brown. These were the three lower orders. The Lion wore a lion's head. St Augustine writes of them roaring. They wore red tunics with purple-striped sleeves, or white, with red-striped ones. The Persian wore yellow with white bands, or white with yellow. The Couriers all had a red tunic, yellow belt and red cloak. The highest of all grades was the Father. He had baggy Persian trousers and a cloak, both red. His tunic colour varied, but his long sleeves had red or yellow piping. It all sounds more colourful than much that we associate with ancient Rome.

I have the sort of body that's easily turned on. After a few more sights – a stable still filled with straw for realism, The House of the Seven Wise Men – a sort of inn – and a glimpse of beautiful frescoes in the one house that was shut for restoration (Roberto had tried to prise open a window but failed) – he was holding me and whispering 'Vieni con mi.' (Coming has the same double-meaning in Italian.) Often men prefer to say 'Facciamo amore' (let's make love). The really crude ones try a sort of playground phrase and say they'd like 'Fare fiche a fiche' – to do cunts to cunts literally. Some ask if you'd like 'Fare cazzo' (to have a fuck). You see the word cazzo chalked up everywhere, often beside drawings of rampant erections, as the word also means 'cock'.

Roberto made the mistake that many men make. He took me across several fields of wet grass to find a suitable place. If I may presume to give a lesson to all the men who're after casual sex – get the woman turned on in the place where you intend to make love, not at a distance. Willingness for a casual liaison is a kind of temporary aberration – if you give someone too long to think, they may well cool down.

When we had attained a place of comparative privacy – the ruins of some old shop perhaps or a poor person's house – we attempted the standing fuck, something I don't greatly recommend. The standing fuck is really designed for the combination of a six-foot woman and a five-foot man with a 180 degree erection. Such a combination rarely occurs in real life. People of more middling heights need to do a lot of awkward positioning. It can be very hard to keep your balance. This was not the most satisfactory experience of my life – a little better than Jean-Claude, but not much.

Roberto seemed quite happy, though. A hundred yards away he was at his *'Vieni con mi'* again. I told him I was *'troppo stanca'*, too tired, which seems as good an excuse as any. Soon he was doing his *'Qui passava acqua'* and being the official guide again. When his watch showed one o'clock he was off, telling me he'd finished work. Guides never make love on their own time.

Maybe it was the wet grass and the dank ruins, maybe it was the tour of the Roman sewers, but after Ostia, ill-health set in. I seemed to have a promising case of 'flu topped with tonsillitis. I went through kilos of oranges trying to ease my throat.

Bones

I took the slow train from Rome to Naples. It's not a particularly interesting journey – just a lot of small places and open spaces. This train was packed with commuters and students. There were several men near me who were so coarse and hideous I felt that they must be Neapolitan. I was wrong though, as they all got off at Latina – the stop which is near the ARSOL-SPA factory. In fact, they looked even worse than Neapolitans. If you ever see a clumsy fat oaf with raging acne, size-20 feet and elbows, tiny eyes and even tinier finger-nails, and he's speaking Italian (of a sort), then he probably comes from Latina.

Once in Naples I decided to try the advice of Matteo the pest of Pompeii. I boarded one of the *Circumvesuviana* trains for Sorrento. He'd told me the prices of various hotels there – even at a few thousand lire more a night, it might be worth keeping out of Naples itself. I walked to the various ones he'd recommended and found they were exactly twice the price he'd said. A few blocks of Sorrento showed me that it was all stinkingly touristy and over-priced. I resigned myself to another dose of Naples. By then it was getting late, so I went straight to the only place I knew.

The proprietor had cut his hair and wore glasses. He looked marginally more respectable – that is, until he sang. The little old chambermaid with styes in his eyes evidently remembered me. He directed me to the best shower –and of course it proved to be stone cold. It's nice to know somebody can remember a guest's tastes for months. Service is not dead in Italy. I could have done without icy water with my April 'flu though. I passed the night in a state

cost a bomb. However much you walk round, you can't find cheap food shops – it's not like other cities in that respect. Anywhere else you can get off the tourist beat and go native. Here, all the backstreets are eerily empty. Do the locals take a train and go to the supermarket elsewhere, I wondered. I dislike a city that's all tourism, however pretty the façade. Nobody in the place seems to be involved in anything except selling goods or services to tourists. Venice is a prostitute. Even the cats *pretend* to be hungry, although there are some perfectly good pigeons walking around.

It's all too perfect – Italy's answer to Portmeirion – one long shopping precinct. I am also rather annoyed by having to walk round endless corners and zigzags to get a short distance from A to B. Give me a straight Roman road any day. I hate crooked places. I didn't know whether to choose the crowded streets or the empty ones. In the end I opted for going with the stream, because there was absolutely nothing of interest in the other places. I had a curious feeling that I was part of the chorus on the set of *Simon Boccanegra* done in tasteless modern dress.

I know St Mark's is beautiful. I know the Doge's Palace is sumptuous. I know that there are dozens of museums to choose from, but I wish, I really wish that the place had some life apart from all of this.

I felt a certain urge to get out. I remembered Casanova's ingenious escape from his prison here – one of the most exciting pieces of narrative ever written. Judging by the Arthur Machen translation, the *Memoirs* are a good work of literature – one that has been most unjustly vilified by jealous critics who couldn't get it up as often.

I spent the rest of that day doing my duty by a few museums. One good unusual one lies in the Campo dei Greci. It has the pompous unmemorable name of the *Istituto Ellenico di Studi Bizantini a Postbizantini*. The curator speaks Greek and Italian and all the inscriptions are in both languages.

If ever you had preconceptions about the size or style of icons, the variety here will disabuse you. Everything is displayed in a simple, light room. There are large colourful complex specimens, far from the pitchily dark Madonnas or saints kissed by the Faithful in even darker churches, that I often associate with the genre. Many of the icons have dozens, even hundreds of figures. The most complex is an illustration of a hymn, 'In Thee Rejoiceth'. It must be a wonderfully complicated hymn, because the picture includes various historic scenes, Stations of the Cross, saints' lives, biblical stories, quantities of angels and all the signs of the zodiac. Every one of the *dramatis personae* has eyes, nose, etc. and they're all facing camera, more or less. It's the painterly equivalent of a Cecil B. de Mille.

If you prefer the simpler stuff, that's here too – a colourful St George in red and yellow on a white horse, busy killing a dragon, all against a gold-leaf background with God dictating in the sky. Another Cretan School picture shows a nice homely Last Supper with various scruffy knives and St John absolutely slumped – more on the table than in Christ's bosom. There's a strange seventeenth-century John the Baptist with feet that look like hinged brass and his hairy coat seeming part of a satyr's flanks. He's quite sinister. There are various Last Judgement and Descent to Hell pictures too, with a very uninhibited use of red and black down among the Damned. One or two of the pictures are badly worm-eaten – like the *Noli me tangere*.

The Spa Towns

The next day I set out to do what I'd come to the north for – begin my search for the Fountain of Aponus. Tiberius once stopped there to visit Geryon's oracle. The lot he drew advised him to throw golden dice into the fountain. He made the highest possible cast. The dice could still be seen shining through the water in the time of Suetonius. I don't know the specific purpose of this oracle – very little has been written on it.

I believe that the fountain must have been at Abano Terme. Suetonius speaks of it as near Padua. Abano sounds like a possible modernisation of the name Aponus. Italian is usually stressed on the penultimate syllable, but locally this place is pronounced *Ab-ano*. When there is a different stress in a word like this, it quite often means it has come from a proper name.

I changed trains at Padua on my way and took a look around. Padua, to me, is a much more beautiful city than Venice. It's a real place, full of real people doing real jobs. It also has trees and parks. (The lack of greenery is my other objection to Venice.)

Padua is surrounded by water too, more or less. The water's in its place though – a narrow river round the town. The streets are still straight. You just cross the water and that's that – it doesn't send you miles out of your way.

My way took me first to the Capella degli Scrovegni, which is in a park that once contained a Roman arena. I'd forgotten that the most famous Giottos were in Padua, so it was sheer luck that took me there. I'd only seen reproductions before – small black and white ones. Now I realise that I have to rank Giotto up there with Michelangelo and Raphael, if not higher. The chapel is filled with around forty paintings – stories of the Virgin and Christ and a Last Judgement. It's mostly in a near-perfect state of preservation. The colour is brilliant. The series has a coherency and fits the architecture so perfectly that this is a worthy rival to the Sistine Chapel. (The American who called me Flavia had suggested I write a poem on the Sistine Chapel. Now, I believe in being obvious in some ways, but that would be going a bit far. I'm not going to write one on the Giottos, either, but I can enthuse a bit.)

Nearby, there's the Chiesa degli Eremitani, with some appallingly damaged Mantegnas. A group of young Italians were trying to get up a madrigal in a side chapel. One of them had brought his viola da gamba to the party. I stood around, hoping to hear the music sung as it should be. They weren't as bad as my Neapolitan landlord, but none of them sounded trained and the female lead was positively bad. I almost felt like offering my services. Renaissance and Baroque music should be sung strongly, not in this wimpish fa-la-la fashion. I know the English often make this mistake – after all, we encouraged Percy Grainger – but I didn't expect it of Italians.

I carried on across the city to my next church, the huge Basilica of St Anthony. This has a welcome relief of loos in the cloisters. The church itself has so many side chapels that it takes a long time to go over. It could be said to provide a history of fresco from the thirteenth or fourteenth century down (I use the word advisedly) to Annigoni. There's a whole chapel full of bloody Annigonis – the other tourists seem to like them. You can buy more postcards of them than anything else. I prefer the paintings by the fourteenth-century Alticherio da Zevio, but I find it impossible to remember his name without a postcard in front of me to prove it. It's surprising how well the different centuries of fresco blend. I suppose it's the different media of various times that has driven old and modern art apart. I find it very healthy that a great old church should continue to commission artists to fill up its spare walls. There's a wonderful continuity and confidence in that. It's very sad that there's no art school in England that teaches the difficult technique of fresco – the most beautiful form of painting. It's even sadder that the government has forced art schools to provide a practical graphical training instead of the old free system. Students will get jobs more easily, of course, but there will be no more original unique thinkers coming out of art courses.

St Anthony's is by the botanical garden, which was shut when I got there. Padua has a long history of medicine. Juliet's doctor came from there – not that he was all that good. You see evidence of medical interests in the local shops. Padua has some health foods. (Unlike Britain, the rest of Italy is still not very interested in unrefined flour, muesli etc. Nobody's told them that their yoghurt should be live, kicking and colour-free.) Of course, there's plenty of herbal knowledge in Italy as elsewhere in Europe – I saw an old witch gathering plants while I was sitting by the Appian Way. Italy, it seems, has just preferred to concentrate on the poisonous aspects. When the health shop boom hits, it will hit in a big way. When it comes, I think it will come from Padua. You can see the first wave there – the pricey honeys, vitamins and a few herbal beauty products.

Near the botanical garden there's a gracious round park – the Prato della Valle. Little bridges lead across a loop of the river on to an island of green divided into quarters and surrounded by statues of everyone who's ever been connected with Padua. It's a good place for a picnic.

I had left Abano to the afternoon. It's a small town – the station was tiny with no one in it. Outside the place smelt terrible in an old-fashioned farmy sort of way. There was a huge dungheap in the first farm that was probably partly responsible. I was met at its gate by a pair of geese – one of whom was jet black with an evil swollen bright red broken nose. Still, I always get on well with animals like that – geese, Dobermans, Alsatians, etc. My mother says they sense a kindred spirit. She only gets on well with broken-down old cats and bitches.

Further on I came to a main road. A large notice welcomes motorists to Abano, telling them to leave the place undisturbed in several languages. It's a very cosmopolitan town, but has little to recommend it unless you want to eat at the *Trattoria d'Artagnan*, *Pizzeria Samurai* or *Gelateria Tropical Sunset*, or shop at expensive clothes stores or have hot mud poured over you in a 5-Star hotel. One of the hotels has a strange bit of statuary – a girl who looks as if she's being buggered by the bloke behind her. Of course, as there's a bit of drapery to confuse the issue, I could be wrong.

155

Perhaps this statue is meant to give the message – you too can do this after a week at our health farm. There are various comic cards sold locally with similar ideas – pictures of fat little men jumping over tennis nets and chasing bosomy women after taking the waters. I'd be tempted to take them myself if only there was some public system. It's all kept for the richest of the rich though. All I could do was get a squirt from a tepid water fountain in a little park.

The shops sell postcards of the local treatments – men or women, with or without woollen combinations, having six buckets of grey steaming mud tipped over them on a couch by a henchman or henchwoman. It all looks rather painful and extremely old-fashioned. I remember seeing a programme once about Italian water cures. Willing victims were power-hosed from a distance or had pipes stuck up their nostrils, in order to have the rheumatism or bronchial troubles frightened out of them. It sounds a bit like the old treatment for hiccups – setting fire to a nightshirt. Give me a bunch of herbs any day. They're decidedly less frightening than these medical torture games. I'm inclined to think they must be some sort of sexual kink.

Of course, maybe I'm missing some subtle pleasure. Who knows? I love saunas – but they're not everyone's cup of tea. I remember two schoolgirls coming and looking through the glass when I was having one. 'Uh, look at that lady,' one of them said, 'She's not moving. I think she must be dead.'

One of the things you can't help noticing about Abano is the sheer age of the people. The very old are held up by sticks and Zimmer frames. The ordinarily old get given matching red bicycles and track suits in pastel colours by their hotels. They're sent out to pedal a block or two for their health, because there's obviously bugger-all else to do in the place. The Germans have the initiative to take buses to see the sights of Padua. Judging by appearances, some of them may well die on the way. They are old-world Germans of the sort you don't see elsewhere. They were probably all too old to fight in the last war. None of them speaks a word of Italian. The woman in the local chemist's talks a mixture of the two languages – prices where the thousands are left in Italian and the hundreds go into German. The bus stops outside her shop. There was a bevy of old ladies in juvenile berets there. They reminded me of Aristophanes' Chorus in *The Frogs* – all they could do to ask the way was croak something that sounded like '*Pad-wa, Pad-wa?*' Of course, maybe they were all aged 110 and remarkable examples of what the cure could do. Another week of it and they might all be jumping over tennis nets and riding bicycles.

There was obviously nothing left of a Fountain of Aponus here. The nearest thing to an oracle is the public weighing machine that gives you a one-line '*Oroscopo*'. This told me that I was a kilo heavier and had an interesting mind. Well you need one, when you're putting on weight . . .

The air in this part was quite fresh, now I was away from the organic bit. There was a good view at moments through sidestreets that petered out into farm-land of the nearby Euganeian Hills.

I decided to go on to Montegrotto, a mile or two further, where there are a few remains of an ancient thermal establishment. The shops were even swisher – full of embroidered silk in very large sizes. The German influence was obvious in catering – there were several *Birrerias* – a word you have to be extremely sober to pronounce. In this town, too, *Salumeria* is spelt *Delikatessen*. I expect Germans who emigrated here could make a fortune selling to their OAP compatriots who won't speak Italian. Before I went there I thought it was only the English who wouldn't learn other tongues – of course, maybe we're all senile too. The senior citizens in these towns are so senior, I feel there ought to be another word for them – *Methuselahs* perhaps. They're probably all expecting telegrams from the Kaiser next birthday.

The excavations at Montegrotto are simply a fenced-off archaeo-logical site. Parts of it are covered in cloche-like structures to save the whole thing turning to mud. It looks like the foundations of several swimming pools and other buildings. This seems to be the only old bit in the town. You can get a slightly better view of it by trespassing in the car park of the Hotel Monte Carlo. Most of the other hotels are called after emperors – maybe they're all part of a chain. By the bus stop there's a Hotel Antiche Terme Tiberio – per-haps that's where Tiberius stayed when he consulted the nearby oracle. It advertises a *Grotta Sudatoria* – a sweating grotto – which sounds filthier and more old-fashioned than a sauna.

Mohammed Ali

That night I took the train back to Rome, hoping to visit the Etruscan necropolis of Cerveteri before returning home.

I was joined in my compartment by a racially-prejudiced Senegalese called Mohammed Ali. He had a fixation about girls with white skin, he told me. Obviously he'd seen me shining from the corridor. I'd just taken my make-up off for the night. Without make-up I look so pale I'm almost phosphorescent.

Mohammed Ali was living in a flat in Venice, where he cooked couscous to save spending in the local restaurants. He was on a sort of modern Grand Tour paid for by his father. He just wanted me for a friend. It was nice to have friends all over the world. I always worry about men who state their honest intentions.

He had not had a good time in Italy. He'd had no sex for a year. He'd got friendly with one Italian girl, but her mother had told him to leave her alone. Prostitutes didn't interest him although there were plenty to be had in Venice. (I pricked up my ears – I remembered reading many lines in old plays about young men being taken to Venetian courtesans as part of their education.) Just last night, he told me, one had come up to him in St Mark's Square and demanded 100,000 lire. That was much too much, he thought, but if he went with 10,000-lire ones he would obviously die. He didn't need sex often and didn't approve of men who did it morning and evening. They would get ruptured, he said piously. One fuck would last him several months. He was a reasonable, abstinent man. He didn't overdo things like some people.

He then went on about how he liked white skin again. He was looking for a white girl to marry. He was wearing a large wedding ring, so I can only assume he was after wife number two. Had I had an African, had I had an Italian, he asked, and were they better at it? I said that I believed people were the same regardless of their skin colour or nationality, but he didn't agree.

I was reminded of what a black girl I was at college with told me. She said it was fashionable among her black friends to score with a white person. She talked of how it had taken her years to see through this attitude and go her own way. Mohammed Ali was old enough to know better – not just to go for white for white's sake.

He'd talked of the heat and differentness of Africa at first with a kind of passion and home-sickness that had made me like him. Now, though, this quest for white skin, regardless of the person behind, made me feel sick. Naively, I expect all women to be feminists, all black people to be anti-apartheid. Life is not that simple.

Mohammed Ali was getting extremely wearing. He kept asking me to help him because he hadn't had sex for such a long time. He had now put the time up to one year three months. I tend to suspect men who can't manage a fuck in that length of time. After all, they only have to be nice to some woman of roughly their own type for an evening or two, then ask. It's different for women – society doesn't allow us to ask. I once tried to cut through convention and asked someone who'd shown a lot of interest, but seemed diffident. I received such a terrible snub that I shall never risk that again. I felt it was the biggest humiliation of my life. Society's still pretty set in its old ways.

Mohammed Ali was sprawled on his seats. He had pulled them across almost to meet mine. You can do that in Italian carriages. He kept going on like a cracked record: *'Dai mi la mano'* – give me your hand. It reminded me of a certain scene in *Don Giovanni*. I wasn't even sure quite what he wanted. Was he asking me to marry him, or did he just want a quick hand-job? If it was the latter – why the hell couldn't he go to the lav for a bit of DIY? *Mano* also means assistance. Perhaps that was what he was after, in the shape of a long-awaited fuck.

The other part of Don Giovanni's record consisted of *'Una volta sola'* – just one time. One time, he said, would last him fifteen days. (So, the few months had gone down.) He only wanted one to remember me by. I was beginning to find his methods of persuasion fairly offensive. I don't like being seen purely as a source of possible relief by someone too mean to pay 100,000 lire to the pros of Venice for it. I also don't like men in search of casual sex saying once will be enough. That's not very flattering. The whole and only point of casual sex is packing a lot into a short time in order to satisfy a physical passion temporarily induced by the good looks of the person concerned. That's how I see it anyway.

I considered telling Mohammed Ali to solve his own problems by masturbating. If I had, though, he would probably have done it then and there – all over my suitcase. Somebody in Rome had almost come in my open handbag, in a bus. I had moved just in time.

I envisaged a scene with Mohammed tossing off and a ticket-collector coming in and blaming me for it. Besides, M.A. must be an unusually sickly specimen if he considered that two times a day would rupture a man and one fuck lasted him weeks or months. I didn't know what a vigorous bit of masturbation might do to him. Maybe he'd pull it right off or go into an epileptic fit or have a heart attack.

I did in the circumstances what any respectable Englishwoman would have done – ordered him out of the compartment and pushed all those predatory seats back. He was on his way to see his brother in Naples. Naples, I reckoned, would really suit a prick like that. He could get himself what he desired – a white girl. Perhaps he'd be charitable about the local problem with baldness.

Pricks

If I thought Mohammed Ali was a prick, the guards on Cerveteri were even worse. I could nominate any one of them quite happily for the Prick of the Year Award.

Cerveteri-Ladispoli is a tiny station on the local line from Civitavecchia. Travelling round on trains you get to rely on the cheap, open at all hours left luggage offices. Cerveteri, though, would not accept my luggage because the zip was broken. The zip had gone the day before on Venice's Santa Lucia station. I have a horrible optimism about what I can cram into small cases, which usually results in disasters towards the end of holidays. My present encumbrance was a black Taiwanese leather affair – a cheap offer from the *T V Times*. It looked quite smart, but was obviously dying on me. It seemed particularly ridiculous of the men at Cerveteri not to take the case as it was actually a good deal less openable by the thievishly inclined than when the zip was in good functioning order. It was stuck somewhere in the middle, with the nylon teeth parting in loops at various points. I had the feeling I was going to have to stay in my dirty clothes till I got home, then take a tin-opener to the thing. Besides, what self-respecting thief would want what I had in there? All the clothes were dirty and very well-crushed – that was what had broken the zip in the first place. I tried asking the station men what I could do, but this elicited no sympathy. I'd hoped they'd say I could leave it *senza responsibilità*, as the man in Rome had said about a carrier-bag of bottles. Of course, the pricks wouldn't let me leave a carrier-bag, either. It wasn't locked, they complained. They also enjoyed telling me that the excavations were six kilometres away, as I shouldered my burden.

I solemnly vow that the next time I go to Cerveteri-Ladispoli, I will take a suitcase full of fish-heads, sealed with a horribly large and visible padlock and chain. The nice thing about Italian left luggage offices is that you pay when you collect, so I wouldn't even have to spend anything for the privilege. The notices tell you that they keep cases for three months before disposing of them . . .

I went across to the bar opposite for breakfast and bus information. That was a mistake – Italians are rarely prepared to admit they don't know the way. My first set of directions led me to a deserted school bus that was obviously without the wherewithal to go anywhere.

My next few queries took me in circles. Cerveteri's necropolis may be well-known in archaeological circles, but it's definitely not on the local shopping itinerary. Eventually I struck gold with an old man and a dog. He was a native of Luxembourg. He not only carried my case several blocks to the bus stop, but insisted on buying my ticket as well. I needed a second bus after this one to get within a mile or two of my destination. The people on the bus were obviously speculating on why I was carrying a case to a no-hotel ancient graveyard. I put them out of their misery by explaining about the courtesy I'd received at the station. They were sympathetic then, worrying about the mile's walk uphill I was letting myself in for. I told them I'd try and make it.

There's a small museum open at Cerveteri. It's in a castle off the main square where the bus terminates. I was able to leave my case while I looked round. Most of the pieces were pottery finds brought down the hillside from the tombs above. There were no mirrors. I'm particularly fond of Etruscan mirrors. These were bronze with engravings of their old gods and goddesses, often with their names written beside. They are the last clues to a more or less lost mythology. The drawing style on them is flowing and rather like Matisse in feel. There's a good collection of them in the Villa Giulia at Rome. The completest explanation of them can be found in C. G. Leland's *Etrusco-Roman Remains*. He owned a number of these mirrors and made drawings of them.

One of the museum's most interesting exhibits is a blackish statue of the god or demon Tukulka. It's from the fourth century B C. He does not look a nice piece of work.

Outside the museum I saw some farmworkers with a van. They

seemed fairly harmless so I asked them the way in the hope that I might get a lift to the top of the hill – a manoeuvre that was successful. I was very proud of myself for getting to the necropolis in spite of the odds. It probably wasn't worth all that effort, but then, I'd have imagined I'd missed something better if I hadn't succeeded. I feel much the same about some men I've chased.

The ticket-seller at the entrance let me leave all my things in his office. I was able to set out with only my handbag and a bottle of water. Like an idiot, I went out of his office and not through the main entrance on to the site. About half a mile along the road I began to realise that there wasn't going to be a way in through the eight-foot fence on my left. I've never been one for going back in life, so I went over instead. I had a nasty moment at the top – the sort that would have left a man singing soprano – but what's an eight-foot gate to an Englishwoman? Inside, I began to find my way around. There were notices up for some kind of advised itinerary. Being contrary, I did this in reverse.

According to D. H. Lawrence's *Etruscan Places*, this graveyard is full of phallic symbols. Now maybe there's something wrong with me, but I couldn't see any. 'Here it is,' he says, 'in stone, unmistakable, and everywhere, around these tombs. Here it is, big and little, standing by the doors, or inserted, quite small, into the rock: the phallic stone!' It's always possible, of course, that some tomb-robber took the lot for his rockery. Lawrence thinks that there must have been a great phallic column on the summit of these tumuli plus others at the entrance to match the seven- or eight-inch ones he claimed to have seen by the doors. These were detachable. The friend he was with, 'B.', took one out of its socket to show him.

Some people see pricks everywhere. Men who write art criticism are the worst – towers, pillars, door lintels, they're all pricks to them – anything that stands up, in fact. It's funny, they never describe anything floppy or unreliable as phallic. A follower of D. H. Lawrence – Christopher Hampton (note the name) – when visiting the same places, even found a field of thistles phallic. Now, if I ever see one like a thistle, I shall run like hell.

A duck (in an Etruscan painting) was another thing D. H. Lawrence equated with his member.

It swims upon the waters, and is hot-blooded, belonging to the red flame of the animal body of life . . . So it became, to man, the symbol of that part of himself which delights in the waters, and dives in, and rises up and shakes its wings. It is the symbol of a man's own phallus and phallic life. So you see a man holding on his hand the hot, soft, alert duck, offering it to the maiden . . . It is that part of his body and his fiery life that a man can offer to a maid.

Now I know why some people like playing with ducks in the bath.

The tombs are bee-hive-like structures, mostly cut out of solid rock, topped with grass. Several of the largest were shut for restoration. The whole place has been cleaned out and all that's movable has gone to the museums. Only the structures remain. The entrances to graves have a shape which slopes like a narrow triangle with the apex cut off. Some of them remind me of the Sibyl's Cave at Cuma. Many of these are also cut out of tufa, although the colour of rock is greyer here. Sometimes you can go down a long flight of steps into an underground tomb. One of these had neon light installed. After the steps there was a long narrow curving side-passage, and in the centre of the main room a square pit which had filled up with oak leaves.

The top of the hill is a labyrinth of tombs with curving grassy paths between them. There are two main old roads in the enclosure – the Via della Serpi and the Via degli Inferi. I didn't come across any serpents in the first road – just lizards, wild roses and gnats. The other road – The Way of the Underworld – is sinister. I was glad I was doing the itinerary in reverse – coming up, not going down. It's the road that the wagons rolled down on their way to the burials. It's still heavily rutted by tracks that are more than 2000 years old. The mud is pressed into long curving ridges that more than twenty centuries of rain have not been able to obliterate.

There were a lot of Italian guided tours going over the place. I think I was the only foreigner to have survived the assault course of getting there. The Italians, of course, had done things the easy way and come by coach.

A number of the tombs have three small rooms leading off a main entrance. Some of the flights of steps down to them are worn through in places. You could see the light coming out of them in the neon-lit underground one.

The Capanna tomb, which isn't particularly interesting, was being visited by what looked like the contents of an Italian old folk's home. I stood and waited as about a hundred old dears trooped out in single file. They weren't quite as decrepit as the Abano Germans, but I still felt that some of them might be left behind.

When I'd seen all that was open – sadly, The Tomb with Reliefs was shut – I got my bags and left. I bought some cards in the souvenir caravan across the way, including one of the museum demon. I'm not a religious person, but as I passed a *trattoria* dedicated to him halfway down the hill, I had the kind thought to dedicate a novena to Tukulka on behalf of the guards at Cerveteri.

All the way down, as I trudged slowly, with bags in one hand and my case over my left shoulder, I could see a man twenty feet ahead, carrying an old-fashioned scythe like Father Time.

The hill where the tombs are situated is beautiful. On any other day, without that load, I'd have loved that walk on a quiet country road flanked by sweet-smelling flat-topped pines and cypresses.

I had blistered hands and had broken out into a sweat of pure agony by the time I reached the square. To crown it all, I had to run uphill in the full heat of the day, for a bus that was about to leave. The bus took me to Civitavecchia. To think that I could have bussed it in comfort from that more civilised station, where the staff would probably have been quite happy to let me leave my ruptured case and unpadlocked carrier-bag.

I took the train to Turin and arrived late, intending to board the midnight train for Paris, then home to England. I ate quietly most of the way – just to lighten my load. I had a lot of scraps of fruit and cheese still in my bag. I had about an hour to kill in Turin, so I decided to go to a café opposite the station and have a hot chocolate. I remembered from the last time I'd taken a train to Italy that it could turn diabolically cold in the early hours as you went through the mountainous area by the border. If you lift the blinds and look out you can see icy streams in the moonlight, which makes you colder still.

The rather swish café opposite the station served the best chocolate I have ever tasted. It is probably more or less as the Incas had it. It is pure melted chocolate with no milk. The waiter just puts a block of it under a steam tap until it liquifies. I could feel some of it resolidifying on my lips. I went at it too quickly and burnt my mouth, which meant I had to have ice cream to soothe the pain, which rather took away the point of the exercise. After all that sweetness, I felt a very English need to brush my teeth, which I did in the station by the water fountain – an exercise that everybody seemed to find amusing.

An Italian boy was dancing on the platform with his radio beside him. He kept looking soulfully at me while we were waiting for the train. His aged father on the seat behind showed only too plainly what he was going to turn into given time. The train came in late on its long haul from Naples. Most of the carriages were packed. I worked my way along fast and got one of the few seats left.

My carriage contained two filthy Frenchwomen, two fat Americans, a girl from Cambridge, a Roman punk, her skinhead boyfriend and me. The customs didn't like the skinhead – he was made to turn out everything, even his cigarette packet. After the officer'd gone, he muttered what sounded like *'Merda di Francese'* (Shit of a Frenchman), which didn't go down too well with the woman next to me. He'd been muttering things to his girlfriend about having a *cazzo*, which seemed a bit unrealistic as she was wearing a leotard and footless tights, topped with a bomber jacket, and we were packed in four a side. I slept for most of the rest of the journey and didn't get cold. The Inca chocolate must have done its trick. When I cleaned up in the morning, I found my left leg was covered in bites. Now it could have been the Etruscan blood-sucking gnats from that cemetery, but I'm more inclined to think it was a flea off the filthy Frenchwoman beside me – she had scratched through most of the night.

It was all change at Paris, and I had the horror of trying to change languages too. It's hard to make your brain cross frontiers as quickly as your body can. I studied French for five years at school, but it doesn't show. I found myself using an incongruous mixture of languages as I changed a little money and got the Metro to Paris Nord. I changed a little more money there, in a simpler way, swapping some English currency for a few more centimes, from the English queue waiting for the fast train that connects with the hovercraft. I had made a sudden decision to pay a few pounds more to get back fast, so missing a collision on one of the Channel ferries.

166

Tarquinia

I had one more trip to make – to see a little more of the Etruscan country and tie up a few loose ends in my research on the sibyls.

I had long wanted to go to Tarquinia, as it's the richest spot for remains of Etruscan painting. There is little of this left anywhere now. Many tombs were filled with colourful paintings, but got damaged by grave-robbers or the damp climate of the area. To enter most tombs, you have to go down steps – these of course also carry down water in the rainy seasons of the year. From the few fragments left, I feel that something good has been lost.

Tarquinia, I was relieved to find, is reasonably easy to get to – well, by Etruscan standards. It's just one stop away from Civitavecchia on the train. You catch a bus for the centre opposite the station. It's mildly touristy – mostly Germans doing the archaeology. The bus delivers you virtually to the doors of the information office and museum.

The museum is fairly small. Near the entrance there's a collection of terracotta sarcophagi topped with long, fat, slug-like men with tiny heads. One of these is labelled as a priest. There are remains of paint on some of them, but most of it has faded off the terracotta.

Upstairs, you can find the prize exhibit, a pair of Greek-influenced terracotta winged horses. These are so pale that they look like a creamy dingy marble. The museum has given them a room to themselves. The other half of the room is taken up with elaborate black vinyl mock-Medieval seating. This has a long semi-circular lattice back adorned by iron bolts at every cross. You are meant to sit on this to contemplate the horses on the opposite wall above eye level.

The rest of the collection is the usual mixture of pottery and votive offerings. The portrait heads are very badly sculpted here. The artists who did them have made the most elementary mistake possible in modelling. They have drawn lines on the faces. A line or wrinkle is made in life by two different planes of the surface meeting. It should be modelled in exactly the same way. Drawing and sculpture are poles apart.

The votive offerings remind me of the bits and bobs in Neapolitan churches. These are full 3-D though, not just reliefs. There's a knee, a big toe, two pricks, two funny breasts which don't match and a small god-knows-what which looks vaguely like a spinning-top. They are all off the Queen's Altar, a plaque tells us. The first set are terracotta, then come bronze bits – fingers, ears, legs, a prick and eyes.

There's supposed to be a collection of tomb paintings in the museum, but the second floor was closed when I arrived. I have a book of reproductions which shows some fine fragments from the walls of the tombs 'della Nave, della Scrofa Nera, del Triclinio, del Letto Funebre, delle Bighe, delle Olimpiadi' (the tombs of the Ship, the Black Sow, the Banqueting Couch, the Funeral Bed, the Chariots and the Olympics).

The postcard-sellers in the town enjoy drawing your attention to pictures from the nearby Tomb of the Bull. There are two cards on offer. I haven't seen the original paintings, so I'll try to describe what's going on from the repros. On the clearer card, a very well-endowed man with his head turned back to front is buggering a very ill-endowed man while a bull with a striped head-dress and a blue prick charges at them. In the other scene, a blue-horned bull sits with his back turned to what's going on. The entwined limbs are rather difficult to read. I think that a standing man is having a woman who's lying on the back of a man on all fours. There also seems to be a string of black sausages tangled up with the three-some. I sent a picture of this to a pregnant friend to cheer her up.

My guide book says that one of these bulls has a human head, although I'm damned if I can see it. It is also named after the tomb's owner – Aranth Spurianas. Maybe it's nothing to do with a cult, just a continental joke about poor old Aranth having horns. Modern Romans seem particularly fond of jokes about people being *cornuto* – cuckolded. Sicilian trains are blitzed with graffiti about it. Aranth brought back to me a mysterious paragraph I saw on the blind of a compartment of a train in western Sicily. The parts I could translate said: 'Professor Monaco – head of a ram, the face of a fucking testicle, the head of a prick, your wife and all your daughters are buffoons and have given you the something-or-other of a head of a horse.' The last phrase reminded me of *The Godfather*. There were three words I couldn't understand – *battona*, *fucio* and *marola*. If any kind reader would like to put me wise I'd be very grateful. Alternatively, a photo of Professor Monaco might explain the deformities.

Tarquinia has an annoying system of opening certain tombs on certain days. When I had walked up to the necropolis – about two miles away – there were just four on view. It's a strange, parched place, with a white dusty path curving between patches of scrub, blasted weeds, tamarisk and dried-up olive trees. The patches of weeds have uninviting notices: *Attenzione vipere!* The tombs have been tiled and rendered, so that they look like a cross between lavs and air-raid shelters on the outside.

The four open ones were Tomba Giocolieri, Tomba Fustigazione, Tomba 5513 and Tomba Cardarelli. The colours used in these paintings are few – two shades of reddish-brown, black and azure – but they have been used to great effect, and have stayed remarkably bright and fresh.

The Tomb of the Jugglers (550–500 BC) has pictures of games and dances and a man with a double flute. The figures are all separate in a frieze. The dancing woman at the side shows a lot of animation. Parts of her costume – the lower edge and sleeves – are diaphanous. Above the figures there's a series of decorative red and blue stripes. In the curved area between these and the ceiling there are two lions – one red, one blue.

The Cardarelli tomb, named after a local poet, has a flute-player, a cither-player and dancers, but it's all faded to shades of brown with the ground of white plaster showing through where the top surface has flaked away. The Tomb of the Flagellation is in a similar state – dancers, a cither-player and an erotic group of two men and a woman. (The last's a bit too faded to sort out the details.)

The really interesting tomb here is the one with the uninteresting name, 5513. The painting within is a vivid, beautiful banqueting scene. It's much brighter than any Greek or Roman fresco that I've come across. It's quite near to the pictures you can see reproduced from the tombs of the Leopards or the Banqueting Couch. At the sides there are music and dancing scenes, trees and birds. It's the central scene that holds your eyes most, with its vivid detail and the brilliant blue-green and brownish-red on white. (The Etruscans had a convention of colouring the men reddish-brown and leaving the women white.) In this picture, the men are lounging on the women's laps. Some historian somewhere will probably opine that the women were courtesans. I just think the Etruscans knew how to enjoy themselves. There's a kind of natural enjoyment of sex in all their sepulchral art — couples leering at each other on top of sarcophagi, etc. Were women more equal in their society? The art makes me think it's possible. It's hard to tell though, when most of the contemporary writing on the Etruscans has been lost. Maybe equal societies get wiped out quicker. The Picts had a rule based on matriarchy — the only descent you can really prove — but where are they now? Maybe oppressing your nearest and dearest keeps you in practice for fucking up enemies. Perhaps, of course, no empire, no nation, can survive more than eight or nine hundred years, a thousand at most. The Etruscans were an old, almost defunct conquered people by the time the Roman historians wrote anything about them. The early paintings are the best evidence of their life and vitality.

There were quite a few Germans doing the tombs while I was there. A baby was being taken to see it all, down the wooden flights of steps. His mother held him up stiffly in front of every painting and pointed to the figures on the walls. He'll probably grow up with some picturesque traumas — or not.

Museum Pieces

From Tarquinia I went back to Civitavecchia and saw the tiny museum there – one that Lawrence had not visited because he'd heard it only contained Roman antiquities.

It's a simple collection that can be looked at quickly. There's a statue of Minerva, who had an early cult locally. It is minus arms and has a gorgon's head on the breastplate. It has a head, but apparently, the *real* one is in the Louvre. There's also a fine statue of Apollo. He's naked except for a quiver. The label says it's a quiver, otherwise I'd have thought it was a circumcised prick of mammoth proportions slung on his back. Maybe it really was a quiver and the top tiny knob is missing. Apart from Time, people love to do things to statues. I have to confess I once put a fruit gum in the eye of a colossal head of Berlioz. I wasn't that young either. Some statues really ask for it. Of course, I wouldn't do anything to a nice Greek god – I'm not that much of a vandal. It's only modern pretension tempts me. It would have been lovely to do something to those bricks in the Tate – like bunging mortar in between them. Recently, my photo was taken in Builth Wells by the statue of the Welsh poet T. Harri Jones, who is lounging nude, opposite the Wyeside Arts Centre. (The statue isn't *really* T. Harri Jones, it's just that everyone says it is, because it's labelled as commemorating him.) His doodah is hacked off every week by the locals and the Arts Council has to send someone with a trowelful of cement to make him into a man again. He's becoming a bit of a wreck with his shapeless grey sausage and two nails protruding from his chin.

Minerva and Apollo are the prize exhibits. The rest of the space

171

is taken up with a three-foot high bronze lion door knocker, a Roman anchor, a rather lined satyr's head and some Etruscan bits and bobs. The votive heads are all right, but the odd breasts are extremely odd – more like pagodas or bell-pushes than the real thing. There are also hands, feet and a prick. This example has badly drawn pubic hairs above it like hieroglyphics waving in the breeze. After Civitavecchia I went to Rome. In the fields between, tomato plums and seagulls were in season.

The next morning I started early for Caserta, remembering the recommendation of the Baian pervert – he of the mother-of-pearl. The Parco Reale is a truly ghastly Baroque place with cascades on the horizon. When you're nearly dead with walking towards these across what looks like a short distance, you can take the bus up and round the fake waterfalls at high speed. The tickets for this are dear, but you can ride the buses all day for the same price if you're masochist enough. The one I was on was packed to bursting with people sucking drippy shocking-pink lollies. A baby rested its bother boots on my bosom and its mother strap-hung above me menacing my nose with her fat, hairy, glistening, Neapolitan armpit at every curving sweep of the journey. I suppose I should have given her my seat.

Anyone who fancies having his cock bitten might well enjoy Caserta. For those with less dangerous tastes, I would recommend nearby Capua – a former capital of the Etruscans and the end of the first stretch of the Appian Way.

You get off the train at Santa Maria Capua Vetere and walk a mile or two to the amphitheatre. There's also a very infrequent bus service from revolting Caserta. The part of the town near the station is very rural, with hens peeping out of doorways and strings of tobacco leaves hung up to dry. The fields around this area are still full of unharvested tobacco, which looks like badly bolted lettuce with pink flowers.

The amphitheatre is in a good state of preservation. I was the only person looking round at first, till a local yobbo decided I needed a guide. Then there was the usual routine of pulling his hands off my breasts, pushing him off my backside, etc. and taking lots of extra turns down flights of steps and on to different levels. He eventually took the hint when I retired into the small museum by the gate. Everything inside was so higgledy-piggledy that it was probably more of a working archaeological school than a museum. Still, there was no one there to kick me out. I could probably have collared a Roman mosaic without difficulty. The place was like the *Marie Celeste* – half-eaten lunch packets on the filing cabinets, a television, a mattress on the table and a lawnmower parked by some unusual sculptures. Two of these were of a type I have not seen elsewhere – Roman presumably, with some of the Etruscan local influence perhaps. The figures were rather plainer and pudgier than usual. I suppose they must have been from tombs. Each of these showed a fat, middle-aged woman seated on an armchair-like throne. The one on the right had a tightly-swaddled baby across her knees like a rolling-pin. The other had two babies – one in each hand, like ice-cream cornets. The ends, again tightly wrapped, pointed into her lap.

Outside the doors there was a fine sarcophagus with crossed dolphins at either end and a strange terracotta of a satyr – some sort of three-foot high water-container, perhaps. The head was bent back flat with an open mouth that connected with the interior. The body was remarkably discreet, with the legs bent back at the bottom to square off the form just above the pedestal.

There was a pleasant little garden here – a graveyard full of ancient steles and inscriptions. It was bounded with tiny well-clipped hedges and hydrangeas. The grass was short and full of red clover. There were a few plum and bay trees mixed in with one or two remains of old graves.

To the left of the gate, away from this area, you can walk round the side of the amphitheatre by large piles of blocks of stone. Some wild fig trees and vines have planted themselves here. Once I got out of sight of the ticket office, I thought I'd do some looting. I started with a few Turkey figs then got to work on a vine. I was horribly greedy and filled my carrier-bag with about four pounds of small sweet grapes.

Back on the main road, one of the handles of my bag went, which wasn't surprising. I decided to wait for a bus to Caserta, instead of taking the long walk back to the station. A local had told me that *il pulman* would arrive *subito*, which in practice means bloody never. When we'd both waited for at least an hour, he started to try to fit me up with various motorists. He kept asking them did they want me and telling them I was very beautiful. I thought it might be a good idea to go and inspect the old Roman gate in the middle of the road, then start the long walk to the station with my collapsing bag. I kept eating grapes and spitting pips to lighten my load. As I examined the dated graffiti about Fascists on the gate, I was joined by another local. As he was good-looking and grades up on what the local pimp was trying to procure me for, I took his proffered lift to Caserta.

Franco was a rock musician, so he said. I always suspect professions like that – but then, he did have transpositions spilling out of his glove compartment to bear him out.

He asked if I would like to see some of the local countryside, go up into the hills perhaps, as we took the scenic route. He had also asked me if I'd like to make love with him. I said no, although I didn't think I'd mind. A girl has to say no for the first few minutes.

Some of the roads in the hills I wouldn't have called roads – just bumpy tracks in the grass between fruit trees. There were a lot of *amareni* growing here. These are a shrivelled sort of cherry more used for ice creams and liqueurs than eating. We ended up outside a deserted farmhouse on Collina Sandra. *Collina*'s a small hill, but I don't know about *Sandra*. This was where he took his girls, Franco said.

We made love. Not only did the earth move, but the condom moved, or rather split and disappeared up me. I don't understand why the government talks about 'safe sex'. One of my friends has had two abortions because of the things. Another has a dear little girl. Probably half the British are here because of them. I was glad that I also take the Pill. I vowed never to use the more expensive brands of condom again. Thankfully, I was able to extract it myself. One of my relations wasn't as lucky on her honeymoon.

When I had sorted myself out and dressed, I was taken to raid the farmhouse fig tree. The place had been deserted for years, Franco said. I didn't *really* need any more fruit, but I managed to force a few down. I was given tips for fig-stealing – they are riper on the upper branches nearer the sun. You pick only those that feel soft. I'd realised that much before. There's another test for full ripeness though – you squeeze the fig. If some milky juice comes out at the top, it's not quite there.

A beer later, back in Caserta, Franco was wondering what he was going to do without me. Presumably he was going to do very nicely without me like I was going to without him. I got the train back to Rome where I'd left my luggage.

Psychologists often talk about *post coitus tristia*. I suppose they must be guilt-ridden and worried they've been unfaithful to Mummy. I've never managed to summon up any guilt about sex. It wouldn't seem logical to me – after all, I'm only making myself and the man concerned happy. What could possibly be wrong with that? Instead of the *tristia* bit, I generally seem to have a foolish grin on my face after sex – sometimes it lasts hours, sometimes days. People tend to look a bit worried and ask me why I'm laughing.

The man opposite me in the train started to show this kind of concern about my expression. He said I must be *sempre allegra* – always gay, 'gay' in the Wordsworthian sense, of course. Actually, at least half of the time I'm a bloody misery. As all Italians will do, he sounded me on where I was going.

I'd decided to take the night train to Reggio Calabria. I had heard that the museum there included some unusual pieces. Riccardo decided to come with me, whether I liked it or not. He said that he was the station-master at Rome and had a free rail pass. Anyway, the situation had one compensation – he was willing to carry my drippy collapsing carrier-bag of grapes. I'd begun to feel that the thing was like a magic purse. However many I ate, it still seemed to be as full as ever. There was an hour or two to waste before the late train I wanted, so I went on a long search for *gettoni* (telephone tokens) with him. I supposed that he wanted to phone some long-suffering wife to tell her he wasn't coming home tonight.

Men love walking me round on futile errands. There were no *gettoni* left in the station machines, so we started on the local bars and hotels. I was rather relieved in a way, because he'd threatened to buy me a nice American hamburger to remind me of home. I'm a very greedy person who can eat almost anything – but anything for me does not include hamburgers or chips.

We traipsed round block after block and he carried the one-handled carrier-bag into all the hotel foyers. Nobody wanted to give him any *gettoni*. Eventually, as the area got more dubious, one of the porters let him use a phone at the end of a corridor.

Now everything was pitch black outside. I saw flights of seabirds going over crying and flapping noisily in the direction of Ostia. Their white bellies looked strangely bright above the lights in the dark city night. I haven't seen anything like it back home in Hastings – a town so full of birds that it ought to be called Gullopolis.

Mercifully, when we got back to Termini, the hamburger bar was closed. Riccardo got me a roll instead and a new carrier from behind the station bar. He also got my luggage back free by endorsing the ticket, which proved he worked round there in *some* capacity.

We shared a carriage with two women who were only going as far as Naples. They were both middle-aged and quite glammed up. They told Riccardo that they had just spent the day in Rome with their lovers. He said about ten times that he didn't believe them.

One of the women was married, the other said she didn't believe in it – she'd seen what marriage had done to her friends and relations. Riccardo argued passionately and horrifiedly on the subject. I lost their drift after a while. They had gone into fast Neapolitan, which is beyond me. I was glad to see that things don't only cut one way in Italy – the women are fighting back. It's happening in Wales too. I recently did a reading tour there and heard a lot of complaints about the macho beer-swilling husbands and chauvinists making the literary groups impossible for women. I think the time's come for men to give us a power share gracefully before they lose the bloody lot.

I slept fitfully, stretched out on the seats. Riccardo snored very loudly and put his pudgy paw on my knee at frequent intervals. I felt strongly tempted to leave him on the train to be shipped to Sicily, but my natural kindness – something most people don't believe I have – won out. We got off at Villa San Giovanni and took the small local train to Reggio. For a station-master he seemed to have less know-how about the Italian railway than I did.

Reggio looked very different from that cold night in Holy Week. The waiting room was empty of lunatics. Outside, much to Riccardo's horror, I let him know that we had a two-kilometre walk ahead. He decided he could just about stand it as long as he didn't have to walk back. The grapes went with us, or rather, with him. He'd been very impressed in a horrified sort of way when I'd told him I'd stolen them. He'd had the same sort of expression on his face as he'd had in the train listening to the Neapolitan woman. He wanted an adventure, he said. (Fat chance!)

Reggio has a boring sort of Riviera resort look — lots of palms and the sea and not a lot else. It seems to be backed by a high mountain which I did not go up in deference to Riccardo's feet. Calabria, he'd said, was so devoid of interest it could all be seen in half a day. Italians like to write off other regions in this way. He kept recognising people on the street. All of Naples goes there on holiday, he explained. When he said that, I realised why he hadn't appreciated my joke about a row of overturned dustbins reminding me of Naples. Any Italian from any other part would have loved that joke. I hadn't taken his mastery of dialect in the train as proof that he came from the town I love to hate. After all, some Romans seem able to talk Neapolitan. It had seemed so unlikely that Roma Termini would employ *one of them* as its station-master.

For a man who only liked Michelangelo and Beethoven, the Archaeological Museum at Reggio must have been a sore trial. Riccardo was under the delusion that I was some kind of expert on antiquities and had ordered me several times to lecture him on all the exhibits. He told me I was a *cicerone, una esperta*. Most of what I said was absolutely elementary. I just let him know what things were made of — marble, terracotta, stone, alabaster, etc. My Italian and my archaeology don't stretch to a lot more. I'm not even certain I was right in all cases. I also let him know that the things upstairs were sarcophagi, not baths. I was quite proud, though, that I was able to tell him that a coin labelled *Panormus* had come from what is now Palermo.

There's a lot in that museum that *I* could have done with an explanation of. Why was that large sarcophagus made in the shape of a foot? What about the thousands of tiny Corinthian pieces? What on earth can you say about an ancient piggy (or wild boar) bank in terracotta, with black figures of Pygmies chasing a hare painted on the side? Why were the female heads around so remarkably ugly? I remarked on this to Riccardo, but he was too magnanimous to agree. Maybe they looked like Neapolitans he'd known and loved.

The site of a nearby nymph's grotto has provided some of the strangest objects. There are tile-sized pieces depicting three women

177

in bed with everything but the heads covered and a head of Pan or a sword in low relief on the middle of the sheet. Perhaps the threesome has some connection with triple Hecate.

Amongst the small pieces from elsewhere, there were several dildo-like objects. One of these had a goddess's head on the working end, which looked potentially uncomfortable. The museum had left this unlabelled. There was also an odd-looking cucumber. The museum had labelled this as a votive offering. Perhaps they were right. After all, the temple at Delphi had a gold radish, a silver beetroot and a lead turnip amongst its treasures. Still, I'm inclined to think that offerings would look like prize cucumbers rather than small, withered, slightly curved ones. But perhaps I'm getting as bad as D. H. Lawrence . . . I thought it advisable to pass these items without comment in my lecture tour.

Apart from the piggy banks, dildoes and ugly women, the museum does have some good big statues – a large sculpture of a boy on a horse on a sphinx, Castor and Pollux on horseback on dolphins – everything seems to be three-tier. Down in the basement, the prize exhibits are kept behind automatic sliding doors – two large bronzes of naked men dredged up from the sea – The Bronzes of Riace. (A) is perfectly preserved. (B) has lost one eye and his teeth. The bodies are absolutely beautiful. I am convinced that male bodies can be that. I've had a lot of arguments on that point though. (Usually it's men who can't see any beauty in the male form.) These two have perfect muscle development from all sides. There's a sense that the sculptor caught a transient moment. Looking at the arms I can see that the two men have just been doing some form of exercise. There's a fractional raising of the muscles and prominence of the arteries. I've seen this particular effect on men who're weight-training in a gym. It vanishes a minute or two after they've stopped exercising.

Riccardo still wasn't impressed, so we went upstairs to the art gallery. I thought paintings might be more in his line. There were two good Antonello da Messinas here – St Jerome and one of three angels appearing to Abraham. These were too small and too primitive for him, though. After these the pictures got worse, and worse, and worse . . . They culminated in a vast nineteenth-century one of very grey cows against very green grass. The grass was very bright and the grey was chalky. In fact, I'd have thought it was done by an amateur if the artist hadn't spent such a lot on acres of canvas and a vast gilt frame.

All that remained was to go back to the station. Riccardo returned to Naples a wiser but not a happier man, and I went on to Sicily with my grapes. I was able to see the crossing this time in broad daylight – but it wasn't interesting. On the other side I caught a train for Catania.

Captain Courageous

Most of the train emptied by Taormina. I've been told to go there by people so often that it's put me off. I was seated diagonally opposite an old man – a very old man – I had him figured for seventy to eighty. When there was space, he moved across and started talking to me.

I ought to have been warned by the fact that he splashed on after-shave first, but then it was hot and sticky, and he did seem so old . . . Paolo asked if I was German. He knew Hamburg well. He seemed very pleased I was English and then started talking it. He knew Hull, London and Southampton. He had been master on various passenger ships, he explained. He boasted of various sea-rescues he'd performed and said he had been in the papers often. He had a lot of cuttings at home. We were nearing Catania by this time. He seemed very polite and respectful and said he was all alone, with no family, and would be honoured if I would have coffee with him so that he could practise his English.

Before the coffee, I soon found out, I had to go through a search across Catania for a car part he wanted. Again, I should have been warned by his thoughtlessness in keeping me waiting here, there and everywhere. And then there was the bossiness. He tried to insist I photocopy my passport, tickets, travellers' cheques and foreign currency notes. He always photocopied things like that, he said – he even photocopied all the bank notes that went through his hands. I suggested someone might steal the photocopies too. Evidently, though, Italian thieves are not thorough enough for this. His system always worked, he said. I just wrote the whole thing off as senile paranoia. He was beginning to worry me about the safety of Catania, though. Taormina was much safer according to him. He knew a very good, very safe, reasonable *pensione* there. He offered to drive me round Taormina first, then take me to it.

When we got to the car and he started driving, it did sound very badly in need of some part or other. It has been said that a man's driving shows his style of sex. (That must mean cyclists are wankers.) Paolo's clapped-out Alfa Romeo made some of the nastiest, strangest *almost* human sounds I have ever heard from one of its kind.

It ground to a temporary halt outside his house and I was taken in to see his etchings, or rather his cuttings. I was still under the delusion that I was on the way to Taormina if the car or the captain didn't die first.

Paolo's cuttings were very impressive. He had had them blown up and made into large picture-sized blocks. He had hung these all over the walls of the hall and the lounge, interspersed with framed master's certificates and various other qualifications in seamanship.

He asked me if I wanted to use the lavatory after we'd surveyed these. I'm a great believer in peeing while you can abroad, in case you can't later, so I said yes. At which point I was handed a plastic carrier bag, which seemed a bit bizarre. I didn't think I could manage to do it in there. 'What's this for?' I asked. Ask a silly question – I had wondered if it was an old shipboard custom. That was for sanitary towels, he said. His lavatory didn't take kindly to such things. I didn't need it, I said, which was what he wanted to know. Anybody who believes that another person is too old for sex just because they look disgusting is making a big mistake. The disgusting ones are the worst. Paolo flung open the bedroom door to reveal a lot of religious pictures and a snapshot of a Chinese girl. He grabbed me and offered me 100,000 lire. I told him I was not a prostitute, but he couldn't understand why I was angry.

By then I'd realised I was trapped. I'd seen a small station a few blocks away – a mile probably. Perhaps I'd be able to remember the way, perhaps not. Perhaps there'd be people to ask. It would be difficult though, carrying luggage. If I could persuade him to take me there by car it would be easiest. I said I wanted to leave.

At this point Paolo started speculating on why I'd turned him down. As I didn't have a period, I must have an infection. What infection did I have? (Presumably he wanted to find out if it was one he had already.) Ah, if I wasn't infected, then I must fear pregnancy. That was not a problem . . . 'So that we do not have one son, I will cover everything – *everything*.' Paolo gestured in the air as if he was laying a sheet across someone. (What did he intend to use – cling film?) 'I want to go,' I said. He told me he must tell my fortune first. He scanned the lines in my hand and told me I had just worked in a night-club. I agreed. I had just performed two poems at the Windmill for TV. I don't think that was quite what he had envisaged, though. All the rest was unhappiness and affairs, which I didn't feel like arguing with. Then, he tried to stick a flower, a big white blossom, in my hair. As it had no stalk it just fell to the ground. I said I wanted to go again. This time he felt he had to watch the weather forecast on TV first.

While this was running he said he would not take me to the station, but to Taormina, where he would buy me a nice pizza and put me up in the *pensione* to prove he was a gentleman. Christ, I hate bossy men. Then he jumped up and pulled out a plush box from behind a few books. Inside the red plush there was a golden coin – a guinea I think – on a chain. I could have this, if I let him make love. The Italians never force women. He just liked his women to love him a little. He didn't ask much.

Not much? The only time I ever loved anyone, that love only came about after months of kindness. Attraction can be instantaneous, but in my view love takes time and can't be bought by material things. I am astonished by the cheek of men who expect it. I remember reading a Russian book once where the prostitutes complained that their clients wanted 'love' for a few roubles. This captain could obviously obtain sex somewhere for his 100,000 lire or his piece of jewellery, but for the bossy decayed old shit to expect love of anyone was outrageous. If he wanted that he might do better by being nice to some old ladies in a Sicilian pension queue.

I was determined to hold out for the station. The thought of being patronised, taking anything free from the *Capitano Coraggioso*, as the papers termed him, made me feel sick. I believed he had more tricks up his sleeve too. If I had been a prostitute, I wondered how he'd have handled things. I remembered his statements about photocopying all his lire notes so that he could prove theft to the

police. People who believe love can be bought are probably capable of anything.

The weather forecast ploughed on. To my horror it was not a brief British-style one. Oh no, this went through all the towns in Italy in alphabetical order with minimum and maximum temperatures, pressures, etc. At that rate it could take hours. I engineered a burst of crying. I can't really cry to order like an actor, but if I'm 99 per cent of the way there, I can decide whether to let go or not. Paolo finally agreed to take me to the station, so that I could get a train to Syracuse and find a hotel. I knew I was going to get there horribly late, but at least it would be the opposite direction to Taormina. Paolo grumbled worse than his car all the way. He was being very patronising, telling me in Italian what problems I had sexually. I kept my temper beautifully until we were on the platform. I had about an hour before my train. When I had found out the time he started up again, in English this time, telling me that I was a nice girl, but I had problems. We were standing by the entrance to the first-class waiting room and there was a good audience of all the local yobboes from his very small home-town where he'd lived all his life. I put my answer into Italian.

No, you've got a problem, I told him, in my best projected stage voice. He turned a little green and disappeared into the waiting room's recesses, which meant I had to raise my voice a little more. I went on to let him know he was a bastard and a swine – an *old* swine. I heard him repeat the word *vecchio* (old) faintly. The blokes on the station were howling with laughter. I crossed on to the middle platform to wait for my train and watched. Paolo could not come out without passing the laughing locals, so he stayed in hiding for the next forty minutes until they all got on the train for Taormina.

After insulting a national hero I wondered if I should head off Sicily quickly, or go into hiding. The thought of Syracuse at 10.30 became less and less attractive. I tried to remember if there were any hotels near the station. Probably there wouldn't be. At the next stop I saw one of the ticket-collectors watching me from the platform. I had hung up a dampish gold lurex dressing gown to dry on a hook by the open window. I had washed it over-optimistically at the last hotel I'd stayed at. I expect the gold cast a slight aura about me because he looked smitten. He got on the train and chatted to me until the next stop. He bore a remarkable resemblance to a poet I used to be in love with – the one whose wife has a doppelganger in Reggio – but actually he was rather nicer. Rinaldo came from Messina and started to extol its virtues to me. I made a date with him for later in the week. He promised to show me all round his home town.

A stop on, Rinaldo was back again. He drew the curtains and started kissing me and had his hand up my skirt to gauge my degree of willingness. He didn't go any further, because he'd have been duty bound to arrest himself for misbehaviour on the state railways. I was quite easily persuaded to return to Messina with him instead of going on to Syracuse alone. This meant changing trains. We waited for the last train back together and had a bizarre conversation. After telling me I was *molto elegante*, which makes a variant on *bella*, he let me know I was very lucky. He could not have A I D S, he said, because he was married. That meant he was healthy. All the boys in Reggio had A I D S, he said. I must never sleep with them. (Do the Reggians say that all the Messinese have it? Perhaps the old inter-state wars are carried on in words these days.) I wondered if his wife was off telling the boys of Reggio she was healthy because she was married.

There was a time when I thought I ought not to sleep with married men. These days I'm less prejudiced. Sleeping with one is decidedly better than being used as an agony aunt – that's a mug's game. In some ways I can respect a man jeopardising his chances by saying he's married. Why should only married liars get lucky? One in three marriages ends in divorce these days, so the institution's not exactly sacred. Of course, if I know and like the wife it's a very different matter.

Rinaldo got me settled into a packed first-class carriage in the train back to Messina. He was doing the tickets, so it didn't matter where I travelled. I wrote postcards and tried to think sexy all the way. As I'd committed myself to an affair with an unknown, I didn't want to cool off by the time the train arrived. I had a certain relish in thinking how like the bastard back home this man was. It made it better that his job was not too high-powered. I planned a little joke for England. I would go up to the poet at the next literary party and say: 'I never knew you took tickets on the trains in Sicily.' He'd look puzzled and say: 'I don't!' Then I'd deliver my gem to make him jealous – he's a dog-in-the-manger type – 'Oh well, it must have been somebody else I spent a night of passion with at Messina.' I could always pretend it was a night of passion, even if it wasn't.

I met up with Rinaldo on the platform at Messina. As usual the carriageful of Italians had found out all my business. They'd enquired who I was writing cards to and why I was going to Messina. I told them I was meeting a boyfriend there at midnight, which made them exchange some looks.

Rinaldo had to fill out endless forms for his overtime and the excess fares on the station. I curled up on the table in the waiting room and watched. I always think that people are unfair when they say Italians are lazy. He'd been on duty since the morning, and now he'd promised to make love all night . . .

Etna

I took the train to Syracuse in the morning. I never got to see the beauties of Messina. Some day, some time, I may do. I'd seen most of Syracuse on my last trip. This time I just wanted to get into the museum and perhaps the Fountain of Arethusa via the tropical aquarium. All I did in the end was buy bagfuls of wonderful cheap fruit – dozens of nectarines, bunches of grapes and tiny pears. The museum had been closed for restoration for years. When, or if, it would reopen, nobody knew. The aquarium closed promptly – half an hour before time – as I arrived. I returned to Catania in the afternoon and found myself a room near the station.

I half-wondered if I'd run into the Catanian pastry-baker I'd met days before on a train to Rome. He had told me that all the men in Sicily would run after me. He looked me up and down, mentioned the ladder in my tights and my broken shoe, and then said he thought that the men in Rome wouldn't chase me. They *might*, but probably not.

The Europensione only had a *camera matrimoniale*, but it was cheap, so I took it. It was in fact rather a splendid room. It had a king-size bed in carved walnut opposite a large mirror in the wardrobe. There was also a tiny bed – for the kid presumably. Another even larger mirror topped the carved dressing table, revealing other angles of the bed. The ceiling was domed and about twenty-five feet high. The centre had a very elaborate loopy plasterwork rose. The walls shaded from cream to pink to blueymauve to cream and pink again in the dome. The woodwork was all light blue. Somebody who'd read a lot of Mills & Boon had really worked hard on the place. I was almost sorry I had to leave early to get the only bus to Etna in the morning.

I had a walk around. Catania seemed busy, trafficky and full of evil louts, but I did not have my bag snatched. It's as dirty as Naples, but the streets are wider so it's much more tolerable. The general effect is scruffy Baroque, but there are nice oddities tucked away – a statue of an elephant with an obelisk on its back cut out of lava (different, if not beautiful) and a Greek theatre. To get into this I had to go through the private door of the local archaeology office in the Via Teatro Greco. (You can't walk amongst the seating.) I stepped through an ordinary wooden door, and was confronted by the theatre – part brick, part tufa, no marble – trapped half-underground in a space between the different street levels, with more modern buildings piled high behind. It's unlike any other of its period, hemmed in as it is by the city's architecture.

In the morning the bus for Etna was packed with tourists and locals. One old Italian had a musical birthday card which jollied things up a little. A friend had sent it to him from Germany. He kept opening it up and the conductor sang some other words to it which I couldn't understand, but which made the old man laugh a lot.

Most of the locals got off at villages along the way. The bus stopped for about half an hour at Niccolosi, so that the driver and conductor could have a leisurely sandwich. The air was fresh and cool there. I got good water from a local fountain. After Niccolosi, the terrain got barer and less inhabited. There was still some vegetation – allotment-like areas with scattered outcrops of bee-hives like tatty wooden chalets on the black ground.

By the time the bus got to Rifugio Sapienza, with its souvenir huts, the land was bare glittering black grit. There is only one bus a day, so you have to spend a few hours on Etna however bored, dirty and tortured you feel.

Etna is traditionally ranked as an entrance to hell. (After a few hours up there, you begin to see why.) Its eruptions were one of the things covered in the Sibylline Oracles.

The local bus to the lower levels is good value. (It covers a sizeable distance for a low fare.) Everything else about Etna's a rip-off. The *funivia* which takes you to the top, or as near as you're allowed to go, is an exorbitantly priced petrolly-smelling little bus which hurtles up the long curving road through the lava fields. You have to hold tight all the way. I let go for a moment and fell on a little French girl who made a great song and dance about it. Curiously, it's nearly all French up there, just as it's almost always Germans on the archaeological sites. Americans only seem to like touristy cities. They give Sicily a miss altogether.

The second bus dumps you at about 2900 feet. That is as far as you are allowed to go. It still looks a long way from the top. You can see a smoking peak several hundred feet above you. The French were wandering round picking up mineral samples from the slopes. You are stopped from clambering up these by sagging cables. There's a persistent wind up at this level, with a strong smell of chlorine in it. It wasn't really cold, though. There was certainly no need of the skiing jackets and wellies some shark was trying to rent out lower down.

I sat down on what appeared to be a huge lump of coke and ate some of the fruit that was weighing me down. The grapes and nectarines had got hot and over-ripe resting above the engine in that cramped little bus. When I and some of the others had got bored with the view of slag heaps and had picked ourselves mini samples of lava, brimstone, etc. we boarded a bus for the lower levels. If you have not hand-picked any bits you can buy them on the bus. The driver has a selection of ornaments which look like satanic turds on varnished plinths.

The next stop takes you to Valle del Bove where you can look down into a valley of mist or smoke and get vertigo. I tried walking across some of the lava fields. This is best done at a loping run if you don't want to rick your ankles. Huge leaps work too. The little French girl I'd fallen on was grizzling, and insisted on being carried everywhere on her father's shoulders. Maybe I had done her a serious injury or maybe she was just too fat to cope with it all. I boarded the bus again. The next sight was from a fairly recent eruption. You had to go down a steel ladder to see the underground grottoes carved by the lava flow. It was cold in a dank sort of way. The guide stood at the foot of the ladder looking up all skirts. Mostly they were huge bums in sensible tweed with long old ladies' pants. Maybe he likes that sort.

The ground underfoot was all ridges and furrows patterned with the marks of molten liquids and metal deposits. Above, out of the grottoes, you had to take large steps from ridge to ridge.

This was the last sight that could be considered of interest by any conceivable stretch of the imagination. The *funivia* took us back to the mini village of varnished chalets. There were two hours more to wait for the bus back to Catania. You have to buy the odd souvenir or cards or something out of boredom. That's their idea. There are honey stalls which give tastings with disposable plastic spoons. The honeys they sell are made by the local bees and come in orange blossom, lemon blossom, eucalyptus and chestnut. The chalets, apart from more turds on plinths, sell jewellery. Lava itself looks reasonably interesting in large gritty grey beads. The coloured bright necklaces are another matter. They definitely don't look like any natural mineral. I had visions of somebody steeping popcorn in vats of primary dyes then fossilising it somehow.

There are also a few rather poor value restaurants. The only loo up here is in one of them. There was a very long queue. When I washed my hands I began to realise just how dirty I was. A stream of black water came off me. I tried my face next – even worse. Oh well, everybody was in the same boat – I might as well go for the *really* dirty bit, my feet. Afterwards I went outside and tried to find a spot that was out of the wind. Every quarter of an hour or so I popped back for a wash. The water still looked as black as ever. I tried to comb my hair, too. A glance in my small handbag mirror revealed that it had become like a mass of steel wool standing out from my head. It seemed to be full of a kind of glittering greyish metallic dust. Even brushing it was painful. I put my head down and worked at it very slowly, starting from the nape. Gradually it began to take on some semblance of ordinary hair again.

The cards they sell in the huts are dramatic. They show pictures of what a volcano *should* look like. The shops also have films on offer – Super-8s of the last eruption. I felt distinctly disappointed that I didn't see anything in the way of a smoking crater. I reckon tourists ought to be warned. They might as well do a package tour of slag heaps of the Welsh valleys. Come to think of it, that would certainly have been less dirty. I left an awful lot of my filth in that restaurant's lavatory without buying a thing there. Of course it serves them right for charging fairly high prices for what looked like uninteresting food.

The way back to Catania seemed shorter. There was less jollity on the bus. Just a lot of fed-up tourists of various nationalities. Of course, the locals were too sensible to go up there.

The First-Class Waiting Room

Back in Catania, I decided to head for Agrigento and the temples. The only feasible way of doing this involved a late-night stop at Palermo and a few hours before an early train.

I sat opposite a young Tunisian on the train. He told me he had just arrived from Malta. He had been a professional boxer since he was seventeen. He was now twenty-one. He seemed exceptionally naive. I watched in amazement as he pulled out a wad of high-denomination lire notes, told me that was all he had and that he was going to keep it safe down his vest. He demonstrated. Palermo was a very bad place for thieves, but he would be all right if he slept with one hand on his cash. He was very sad because his mother was in hospital. I asked if it was serious and he said it was. Would I like to see a photo? He got one out of his almost empty travelling bag. (How do some people travel so light?)

His mother looked Persian – middle-aged, quite good-looking. I told him she was beautiful and he agreed heartily and seemed greatly comforted. He was talking a mixture of Italian and French mainly. He knew a little English too. He seemed anxious to make friends with everyone in the train. He borrowed newspapers and found out where everybody was going. Some of them, I could see, took an instant dislike to his brand of open, jolly friendliness. I rather liked him, but couldn't help feeling he was bound to be one of life's victims. I could see him as a punch-drunk boxer in ten years' time – one who hadn't put anything by for a rainy day and had been rooked by managers and agents.

Water was short in Sicily that year, so they'd turned it off in the

Ladies when I got to Palermo. I went into the second-class waiting room to rest for two or three hours before the next train. An official came and suggested everyone there went in the first class instead as it was more comfortable. I was glad, as I had longed to get a proper look at that beautiful example of gilded nineteenth-century Baroque with its painted ceiling. I found on touching the walls that the marble there is fake, but it is well done.

After about half an hour there were two new arrivals. They couldn't have come off a train, because all the trains had finished for the night. I decided that they must be gay prostitutes. I had been told that Palermo has the most beautiful ones in the world. These two were certainly very beautiful. One of them was blonde and exactly like the angel on the right in Raphael's fine fresco of the deliverance of St Peter in the Vatican. He was wearing a short-sleeved loose white crêpe de Chine shirt with shoulder pads and a diamanté brooch at the throat above tightly-waisted loose black trousers. His friend was the spitting image of Rossetti's model Susan Morris, with a cloud of black floating Pre-Raphaelite hair. His clothes were all skin-tight. He had a broad elastic belt with a six-inch clip fastening at the front round his small waist. His trousers were cut very tight and his shirt even tighter – it was a sort of silk jersey white and navy fine striped top with cutaway shoulders. I felt profoundly jealous – I was at my worst after Etna – even on a good day, though, fresh from a sauna or with my hair newly done, I could never aspire to that level of grooming. I've hardly seen anyone who could. The nights in Sicily seem as hot as the days. But that pair obviously never sweated. Their arms were hairless and flawless. Their eyebrows were perfectly plucked and they had just a little touch of make-up – matt foundation, eye-liner and mascara and lipstick – all natural shades to make them a little bit more right. I've seen a lot of top film stars in my time working as a film extra, or when I was an usher at the Old Vic, but none of them were *that* perfect. I could only admire the sheer beauty of this pair and hope they earned a lot.

I watched them, taking odd looks from time to time between pretending to be asleep. They lay back across several seats fanning themselves, occasionally laughing and talking quietly to each other. About every half an hour, perhaps in response to some signal at the door, which they were near, they would exit and then return in a quarter of an hour or so, which made me think they were probably not having as easy a life as they deserved. In fiction, they would certainly have been kept by an Arab prince and had favours lavished on them. Life's not like that though. Beauty has never been a path to success in love, lust or prostitution. Whatever the cosmetics and perfume manufacturers tell you, being well-groomed doesn't bring any rewards either. There are plenty of sexually-satisfied, content slobs and absolutely nothing happens after a Badedas bath.

An hour or so into the night, a tall railway policeman came in and demanded a look at everyone's tickets and papers – everyone's, that is, except the prostitutes'. My ticket wasn't first class, so I expected to be chucked out nastily like the others, but that didn't happen. I soon realised what was going on. The policeman was racially prejudiced. The Tunisian boxer was ordered out most contemptuously of all. He wasn't even allowed the second-class waiting room. He got to sleep on the platform. I saw him there, smiling even in his sleep, too good-humoured to be hurt as anyone else would have been by that kind of treatment. The equally harmless Japanese tourists with their cameras and piles of luggage were allowed the use of the second-class waiting room. My natural pallor and a British passport earned me a share of the first-class waiting room together with the beautiful prostitutes.

Italy is in the position of Britain a decade ago as regards discrimination. Outsiders are seen as people who could take work away. Many Italians even boast about being *razzisti*. It's strange when there is so much resemblance facially between, for instance, Tunisians and southern Italians. White plaster casts of ancient sculpture have perhaps distorted our idea of the classical world. The remnants of painting and mosaic that still exist are probably a much fairer guide and generally contain a less idealised form of the humans within them. Looking at ancient paintings I often feel that the Greeks and Romans of those days looked like some types of African. I've read some works that had been translated from Ethiopian literature which overlapped with the classical writers and historians, but that's too little to go on. Perhaps, also, the cults of the sibyl had something in common with African witchcraft – in their prophetic frenzy. There was a sibyl in Libya. There are still remains of an oracular grotto beneath the ruins of Carthage, I am told. Silvius Italicus contains an account of a visit to this sibyl as well as the one by Lake Avernus.

The oracle was under the temple dedicated to Dido on the spot where she had died. It was hidden in the shade of yews and pine trees. The temple contained statues of Belus, Agenor and Phoenix – ancestors of the race, according to the poet, but perhaps names with demonic connections as well. There was also a statue of Dido with her husband. During invocations the marble of Dido's face sweated. The priestess who called up the gods of hell and the dead was of the Massyli. This tribe is sited now in Algeria. The priestess had streaming hair and Stygian dress. (I had a phase of Stygian dress myself while about to enter art school – black lipstick, bare feet, trailing skirts and a bat necklace.) The passage mentions horrid rites, but doesn't say what these were. The Carthaginians, of course, did go in for a certain amount of infant sacrifice. The place sounds volcanic in the description – earth tremors and flames. I don't know if this is possible from the terrain. It must have been a large complex if the description is accurate – 100 altars are mentioned.

Fishers

The train to Agrigento was slow – one of those that stops every-where so that the station officials can have a chat.

Agrigento has the most monumentally foul suburbs invented by man – tatty tower blocks, ten storeys high, backing on to the railway line at various odd angles. The station itself is unusual in that it is about a couple of floors below street level. Outside it's an unwelcoming place. None of the bars seem to serve any food. There weren't any shops in that part of town either. I took a bus to the temples. These seem to be permanently open and free. There was a notice up about hours, but I was before time and there was no gate or admission office to stop me. Nearby there was a bar with flies which served the worst coffee I'd had in Italy. I almost wondered if it was British-run.

There were a few souvenir stalls too – mainly selling guides and tiny plaster casts. As far as I could tell from my brief visit Agrigento is touristy and yet without much of a corporate identity as a town. It straggles. Those with cars see it best – straight to the temples and then out into open country. The temples are almost in the country in fact. You have a vista of unabated farmland, fertile field after field going into the distance from there. It doesn't look short of water in this part anyway, nothing is dried-up. It's a bit colder than some parts of Sicily, I think. All the trees looked less far advanced – most of the figs were unripe – I'd have nicked some otherwise, and the prickly pears were just about starting.

The main section of temples is mixed up with what appears to be a villa and private gardens. Parts are inaccessible. There are numbers of old gardeners wheeling barrows of refuse away and

194

tending the fruit trees. One of them cut open a prickly pear for a German girl who had never seen one before. There's a small museum with a few fragments in it, near some Christian graves, most of which are in the gardens where you can't visit them. A lot of people seem to have peed in the bits of ruin you can visit. Most of the large impressive temples are in process of restoration, so you can't get all that close. They stretch along a mile or two of road. I had looked at a plan outside, but it's remarkably difficult to tell which is which and what gods they're dedicated to.

The open gateway out at the end of the temples led to another souvenir stall. From there it was a long walk to the nearest bus stop and the road back to the station.

By the early afternoon I was heading for Palermo again. As the crow flies, Agrigento and Marsala are not that far away, but the section in between is more or less without trains. My map has a dotted line in that area which probably means a bus perhaps once a day. The train timetables in the station show a train that goes about one stop along the way, after that who knows?

It took me most of the rest of the day to get to Marsala via Palermo. I still had my Etna dirt intact and I was longing for a shower. Dirt evidently doesn't put Italian men off. The stop before Marsala a yob with a head of curls made a pass at me. I'd almost swear he was the same yob I said 'Va fa 'n culo!' to the first time I visited that place. This time he closed the carriage door and pulled down the blinds in spite of my protests about the heat. I knocked him flying and he left saying reproachfully that Italians never used force on people.

When I got to Marsala I started trying to decipher the timetables for the tiny stop of Raggatisi Birgi, as I wanted to try that difficult walk to Motya if there was no other way of getting there. One of the locals helped me find the info I wanted. I was so tired I started arguing about the direction of the train.

I fixed a date for that evening with Gerlando, the man who'd helped me, then booked into a hotel. I was as dirty as I'd thought, I decided under the shower. I washed the dress that had been up Etna too. In fact, I washed it several times while in Italy and several times back home. It still seems to bear an aura of Etna with it. Luckily it was only an old one I'd had since I was fourteen. I haven't got bigger, only taller since those days.

I went out for a pizza with Gerlando a few miles from Marsala. He worked as a bank clerk in Trapani, he told me. He was in his early twenties and had just finished a law degree in Palermo. I told him he would probably be the bank manager in ten years' time, at which he was offended. He planned that for ten *months'* time. That seemed highly unlikely, I thought, unless he had Mafia connections.

The pizzas were very good – overflowing with baby squid and large prawns. We went walking on the beach beside the restaurant before they arrived. Gerlando had a bit of a sea-fixation. He talked of long lazy days on the beach and tried to teach me an Italian pop song about loving the smell of the sea on someone's skin. His voice was so tuneless that it was impossible to guess what notes he was trying to sing.

Gerlando stopped on the way back at what was evidently the local fucking spot. It reminded me of something from an American movie about Fifties kids. There were all these cars drawn up on the sandy edge beside the sea, just off the road. Each car had a couple and there were odd noises coming from some of the open windows.

Before we got down to anything much he talked a lot. He even cajoled me into giving a rendition of *'Plaisir d'Amour'* to prove I could sing after my attempts at copying his song. I felt somewhat foolish sitting there belting it out – my voice projects a lot – with my blouse undone. (He had got that far.) Perhaps he had a thing about half-clothed opera singers. Anything's possible where male fantasies are concerned.

Apart from my voice, Gerlando admired, or rather, was impressed by my muscles. I had told him I did weight-training. He felt my biceps and muttered *'Madonna mia!'*

Unfortunately, he turned out to be one of those frustrating Italian males of the sort that's had sex with so many contraceptionless girls that he's perfected the technique of withdrawal. He'd talked of liking to have many girlfriends, not just one. Sooner or later he was going to *'get caught'*, as some men like to put it. That was obvious. Of course he would need a wife as a bank manager. Bank managers have to have wives to prove they're not gay or a woman.

I thought I heard a noise at this point. Gerlando said it was only the fishermen and they weren't looking. They are now, I told him, waving at them. Fishing off Marsala is a strange, primitive business.

A couple of men, or a man and a boy, glide up and down by the shore in a shallow-bottomed boat, passing a light over the water and hauling in their nets. The light is often left standing in the stern of the boat. They do their fishing semi-naked, just wearing a pair of briefs. Often, you can see the light revealing a pair of legs topped by snowy pants or swimming-trunks. The light is only strong enough to travel up to the boy's waist. It's a wonderfully funny comic-ghost effect as the boat glides with a faint swish through the waters. We couldn't help stopping to watch every time it happened.

Motya

Next morning I headed for Motya. I had a swimming-costume on under a very old skirt so I could get wet with impunity if I had to walk through the sea. I got off at the tiny station of Raggatisi Birgi, much to the station-manager's surprise. He asked my business. Obviously nobody else had used his station for a long time. A small plane passed over – not far over – for the nearby airport. Everything else was countrified. He offered to drive me to the departure point for Motya, several kilometres away, as soon as the next train had passed through. He had not heard of the causeway through the sea. There was a boat service as it was summer, he said.

The boat runs from the *Saline* or salt pans. These are swimming-bath-like squares of shallow sea water bounded by thin causeways. They are allowed to evaporate and then the salt is piled up on the mainland in huge masses, the shape and size of long low huts. Some of these are roofed in the middle with red tiles. There are one or two small mill-like buildings too, perhaps generators. The men who work there bike along the narrow causeways on tatty old boneshakers. It's a bizarre landscape, not like an industrial one – more like a funny village on snow-covered ground. It looks impossible on a summer day. I'd picked the hottest day of the year in the hottest part of Sicily for my expedition.

The man with the boat waited for a while for other trippers to turn up, but nobody did. He had two mongrel dogs who jumped in the boat with us for the crossing. He kept feeding them grapes. I tried this elsewhere on other hounds – Italian dogs are happy to swallow grapes like chocolates, pips and all. I haven't attempted it with an English one yet. The sort of grapes you get in England probably wouldn't be any temptation.

The water was perfectly clear and shallow all the way. The man steered the boat carefully. The little piers on each side of the water were covered with tyres. It was a cheap trip. You pay a return fare, because the boat is your only way of getting back. The last one leaves at lunch-time. The archaeologists on the island have their own separate arrangements.

I had a photocopied map with me which impressed the boatman. I had got it from a book called *Motya, A Phoenician Colony in Sicily*. This is a fascinating account of the history and archaeology of the island. It was written by Joseph Whitaker, a member of one of the local wine dynasties. It had been his life's work to buy the island, piece by piece, excavate and write about it. It's one of the best archaeological books I've read. The island hardly rates a mention in most guide books.

Motya is mainly interesting because it retains a few traces of the Phoenicians. Most of the archaeological evidence on their original territory has been wiped out by successive generations of Greeks, Romans, Byzantines and Mohammedans. Only fragments of one Phoenician writer, Philo of Byblus, have come down to us, and he wrote in Greek.

The Phoenicians were a Semitic race. Originally they inhabited the shores of the Persian Gulf before migrating to the eastern edges of the Mediterranean. Between the seventeenth and thirteenth centuries BC, Phoenicia was connected with Egypt, and Sidon was its chief town. When Egypt declined, Tyre took over this role. By the ninth century BC Phoenicia was a tributary vassal of Assyria. Later, it was overrun by Egyptians and Babylonians. After a thirteen-year siege of Tyre, Phoenicia became a dependency of Babylon under Nebuchadnezzar from 538 to 528 BC. By 527 she was part of the Persian empire. In the middle of the fourth century she became independent until Alexander advanced into Syria in 333. Tyre alone hung out for a while with another siege. After this the Phoenician identity merged with that of the Greeks and later the Romans.

Phoenicia extended along the seaboard from Mount Carmel to within a few miles of Laodicea. It was a fertile land hemmed in on the east by mountain ranges. It had excellent harbours and good fishing. There was an abundance of the murex shellfish used in making the famous Tyrian purple. The Greeks, it is said, derived their weights and measures and also their alphabet from the Phoenicians. Perhaps, though, *they* in turn got it from elsewhere. The Phoenicians were essentially traders. They sold their own textiles, metalwork, glass and pottery, plus ivory, hides, ebony, feathers and precious stones from elsewhere. They excelled at engineering. Their architecture was based on monolithism, unlike the Greek. Mostly, now, there are only foundations left, as the superstructures were of wood. Some of these have vast stones, like those thirty-nine feet long and seven deep under the temple at Jerusalem.

The Phoenicians made a number of small colonies in Europe while on their voyages. Most of these were on islands, promontories and headlands. A few were started in Sicily sometime between the eleventh and ninth centuries BC. When the Greeks came to Sicily they left most of these and concentrated themselves in Motya, Selinunte and Panormus (where Palermo now stands).

The colonisation of Motya dates back about twenty-eight centuries. By the fourth century it had become a dependency of Carthage. It was a rich, desirable town, with fine houses several storeys high and a successful textile trade. In time, Dionysius of Syracuse became interested in acquiring it. The Motyans commenced their defence when he was on the opposite shore by cutting the causeway that linked them with the mainland. At first the Carthaginian general Himilco was able to give help by destroying the warships that were stationed by the island. Dionysius, though, successfully attacked by shifting his ships over land or through the shallows – eighty triremes in one day – so that he could sail on his enemy from deep waters. The water of the Stagnone, a sort of lagoon almost which contains Motya and other less historic islands, is shallow, and rich in a kind of algae which makes the dragging or pushing of boats possible without too much damage. Greek boats of the day were provided with wooden rollers, too, for occasions like this. Himilco sailed back to Africa, realising he was outmanned, and left Motya to her fate.

Dionysius's attack was carried out from the north of the island, where the causeway connected and the water is shallowest. In fact, this causeway does still exist, just about. It was what I had planned to walk across on. The depth of water above it varies slightly, but is not drowning depth. The beginning of it is a little hard to find. When I had walked round to this part of the island and seen the vestiges of the old walls and that gateway, I discovered it with the help of one of the island's archaeologists. There is soft mud at the water's edge. You have to wade out about a hundred yards perhaps before you see a series of regular squared-off whitish stones beneath the surface. There are a few distant markers sticking up from the sea to show the curving route in the opposite side. I walked along it a little way, but it's easy to slip or tread on the odd barnacle, so I turned back. I was glad that the boat service was there for my return crossing.

The story of Motya's end is a sad one. Dionysius brought battering-rams and war-engines across the causeway and up to the north gate. The Motyans threw down burning brands and pitch-covered tow to set fire to the wooden siege towers. Six-storey towers were used for this battle to be on a level with the houses.

After this first encounter the islanders abandoned the defence of the outer walls and shut themselves within the houses and buildings inside, closing off the gateways. Fighting went on daily, with the siege towers being brought up level with the flat rooftops and upper storeys. The Greeks retired each evening after the trumpet signal, or so the citizens thought. After days of fighting, Dionysius sent in a small band of men by night. All was soon over. The inhabitants were massacred – the old, the young, men, women, children. Eventually Dionysius called a halt to his men and got a public crier to announce that all who wished to save themselves must take sanctuary in the temples of those gods that were revered by Greeks and Phoenicians alike.

The booty of the town was vast – gold, silver and costly garments. The remaining Motyans were sold as slaves. The few Greeks who had fought on their side were crucified. The island was then garrisoned.

It was retaken by the Carthaginians the following year, but the town had become such a wreck that it was soon abandoned for Lilybaeum, the westernmost point of Marsala. There is a theory that Dionysius never pursued his successes against the Carthaginians because of an oracle he had once received. He had been told that his death would occur after he had overcome those who were stronger than he. The prophecy was fulfilled differently – he died after over-celebrating his success as a writer of tragedy. His rivals were poets. Take note all those who win poetry awards by pulling strings. The Irish believe that poets have the power of cursing. They may well be right.

Motya was never really recolonised. A few people lived there from time to time. A lot of the original stonework was used to make humbler huts, or carried off to the mainland. Under Norman rule the island passed into private hands and then to the Church. Eventually the town owned it and sold bits off in the eighteenth century as smallholdings, salt-pans, etc. There was a small hamlet tenanted by farmers who grew corn, figs, grapes, olives and almonds. The island was once celebrated for its wine and figs. It is still covered with fields of vines. A small church was built there which had in it an oil-painting showing the village being visited by a water-spout in 1857. No fatal result occurred – owing, it is said, to the interposition of the Virgin and Child. I could find no trace of this church.

Most of the remaining ruins are the old burial grounds. These are still being excavated. There were also burial grounds on the mainland at Birgi, which were used by the Motyans to avoid filling up their small island too quickly. One of the two cemeteries on Motya was used only for domestic animals and babies – probably sacrificial offerings. The remains of very young human infants, lambs, kids, calves, dogs, cats and one monkey were found there.

A central part of the island, once an important quarter, is called *Cappidazzu* – Sicilian dialect for *cappellazzo*, a large hat. This name was started because the spot is supposed to be haunted by a spectre in a large hat, the ghost of a hermit who once lived there.

A plump archaeologist elected himself my guide round this part and the other bits of ruins. Most of what you can see is the foundations of the old walls and small sarcophagi or cineraria being brought out from the graveyard areas under excavation. There is also a small mosaic of a primitive type done to a Phoenician design with black and white pebbles, as some of the earliest Greek mosaics were. At the southern end of the island there is the Cothon, which looks like a kind of cement swimming-bath, but perhaps once had a use as a sort of internal harbour or dry dock. It has recently been partially dredged out as former ages had been using it as a salt-pan.

The archaeologist insisted I share his ancient iron bike for this tour round the island. I felt very undignified – and worse, unsafe – balancing on the crossbar as he pedalled along the uneven roads with outcrops of stone and hanging branches. The tour culminated in a cup of coffee back in his hut. He had a sort of large thermos full of water by the stove, which he had brought over from the mainland. Motya's not having water of its own is of course one of the reasons that contributed to its final desertion. They had rain cisterns and spring-water brought through large lead pipes from the mainland. Now even these options seem to have gone. The archaeologist also had a bucket of sardines on ice with him. As the pièce de resistance of my trip I was offered a look round the house of the English family who owned the island. I hoped this would contain stuff from the closed museum, but it was just an ordinary house, half-built. It had several floors. The upper floors had rickety temporary wooden stairs which began to make me lose my nerve. There was the odd bit of love graffiti on the walls. The painters and plasterers hadn't finished everything off yet. Inevitably I was shown the bedrooms with a few grabs. I wasn't interested though: he had a horrible, bare, sun-burnt pot-belly.

Whitaker's book had described the contents of the museum at its start. I would have rather liked to see the coins. Perhaps they had been shifted to the newly opened collection in Marsala. Greek and Roman coins have a kind of vigour in their sculpting or drawing, whatever you call it, which seems lacking in later specimens. The portraits of emperors look more real. Of course, many old coins do not have a ruler on them. Motya's own coinage had female heads or gorgons on the front, crabs or palm trees on the back. There was also one sole coin from Lilybaeum described in the book – this had a head of Apollo on the obverse, a tripod on the back. This seems like further evidence for the existence of a sibylline cult in that area.

I had about an hour before the boat left, so I thought I'd go for a swim to cool off. There were about a dozen trippers on the island now. Most of them had come there for picnics rather than archaeology. One family had bags of shellfish that they had gathered.

I tried to swim first in the Cothon, but found myself entangled in long trailing bits of weed. I scratched my ankle on a stone edge in my haste to get away from whatever it was. The best swimming water seemed to be at the end of the jetty the boat used. It was just about deep enough there, but a couple of boys kept diving over my head. They'd parked their baby sister in a rubber ring, bobbing up and down like a cork. *'Come ti chiami?'* (What's your name?) she asked me as she floated near. Italian children are fearlessly friendly with strangers. I expect they are less in danger of being interfered with in a country where people like them and also like having sex with other adults. British men are very prudish about showing they want sex with anyone. Given that kind of attitude it's probably easier for them to mess around with their own daughters. Of course, keeping it in the family is also cheaper. They never have to buy their girl a drink. The family allowance keeps her in orange squash.

I was given a lift back to Marsala by an Italian couple. They were on holiday, going round all the sites in Sicily at speed. Their back seat was littered with colour brochures of museums.

That night I had another date with Gerlando. This time we ate outside a different restaurant and got covered in bites. I like the Italian word for mosquito, *zanzara*. It seems absolutely right.

Afterwards we went to see our friends the fishermen, as he put it. Later that evening Gerlando made one of those strange remarks that always make me feel that I am still a long way from understanding male psychology. He muttered that he would like to finish in my mouth because I have beautiful hair.

Cults

The next day, before I caught my train, I visited the Enoteca and had a lot of samples for breakfast. It wasn't my fault, the man kept pressing them on me – tot after tot of older and older wines until they all tasted exactly the same. I bought a bottle out of shame.

Then I went next door for another look at the museum. One thing had been added since my spring visit – a display about the Sibyl's Grotto. There was an eighteenth-century French travel book lying open at an odd three-part engraving – a plan of the grotto. The main picture was of men carrying slabs of rock to build it. Beneath this there was a procession of robed worshippers leaning over a square well. They seemed to be mostly women – a line coming and going. At the side there was an illustration of the mosaic design. The case also contained a watercolour showing the remnants of the Christian paintings in a more complete state. The cards beside talked of the grotto as the residence and tomb of the *Sibilla Sicula*, the Sicilian Sibyl. That was certainly one more than in most traditions. The church above, they said, was built in 1555. The bit of mosaic underneath, in the grotto, was of a third-century B C African design. The cult was probably an oracle of the water, attached to another cult, that of Apollo. The grotto was used later by Christians. In local tradition the miraculous powers of the spring were remembered. But what *were* those powers?

I tracked down the French book later in the British Museum. (It's about the heaviest tome I've ever had to pick up and stagger to a table with. The assistant said: 'Can't you get something small instead?')

Houel, the author and engraver, wrote of the celebrations of St

John's Day, still preserved in his time. Lilybaeum, he said, was founded before the Trojan War. The town's name came from its being opposite Libya. (I don't vouch for this etymologically.) The sibyl was the one from Cuma that Aeneas had visited. She came there to die.

The grotto, he said, was eighteen feet deep. He talked of the wells as both being fresh water, connected by a canal cut beneath the room and going out to sea.

On St John's Day, the wives of the town came to consult the prophetess. She relived for them in the water which collects at the end of the grotto. They used to ask if their husbands were going to be unfaithful that year. Young girls would ask if they were going to get married. They drank the water, then their exalted imagination made them speak certain words in front of the opening of the canal. The women heard replies and interpreted.

Cicero said that the Pythian prophetess at Delphi was inspired by the power of the earth and the sibyl by that of nature. Plutarch wrote that her spirit mingled with the air, and that it should always be borne onward in voices of prophecy. Her body, though, would transform within the earth and grass would spring up from it that the animals reared for sacrifice would eat. This in turn would transform their inward parts and colours, so that these could be used for prognostications. There are no sacred beasts around Lilybaeum now, if there ever were. There's not even a stray cat in that area.

My only other information on the worship of the sibyl in Sicily turned up in Whitaker's book on Motya. The Latin and Greek historians, apart from a vague mention of a cult surrounding a spring in Diodorus's works, say nothing. I suppose it took a local man like Whitaker to know anything about it, and one of another stock – English – to divulge it.

This is what he wrote:

On this stretch of open land, not far from the sea-shore to the westward of Marsala, and outside its walls, stands the small church of St. John the Baptist, erected on a site above a grotto hewn in the rock, where the Cumaean Sibyl is said to have dwelt and died, her remains being buried on the spot. A spring of water is to be found in a small well in this grotto, the waters of which were supposed to impart the gift of prophecy to those who drank of them. Even to this day the spot is held to be sacred, and is visited by numbers of the Marsala townsfolk on the Eve of St. John.

The well, Whitaker writes, is called Lilyba. It was well-known among the ancients and gave its name to the promontory and the city.

I gathered from the Marsalans I talked to along the way that they still went to the grotto for the festival. They are quite a pagan lot. *Ferragosto*, the important Italian festival for the Assumption of the Virgin, is celebrated here with fires on the beach. Every Saturday – the traditional day for a witches' sabbath, one might say – young people dance about fires in the night. Perhaps that relates in some way to the far-back Phoenician blood. I don't say I have any of that, but when I was a small child I used to like to build altars to Baal, simply because I felt the Bible had discriminated against him.

I was puzzled at first that the church on top of this old site should be dedicated to John. Gerlando had told me that he was the patron saint of Marsala – but was that true? This church is *outside* Marsala's walls, and the cathedral isn't dedicated to him. In most cases when the Catholic Church absorbed old cults and took over temples, they named the new building after a *similar* saint. In what way does John the Baptist resemble the Sibyl of Cuma? I think there are three points which explain this association: they were both prophets and spoke, according to tradition, of the coming of Christ; they both used water in their rituals; they both have a connection with a sun festival. St John's Eve is at the summer solstice, traditionally a time for fire rituals. The sibyl was the spokeswoman of Apollo, his vicar on earth, *a voice crying in the wilderness.*

I took the train to Trapani and found I just had time for a bus to Erice before the long journey to Rome. Erice is the classical Mount Eryx, where there was once a world-famous temple dedicated to Venus – a splendid, white marble affair. I wanted to see what little remnants remained. The bus climbed slowly round and round a hill until it deposited us all in a square at the foot of the town. It was the afternoon, so everything and everyone but the postcard-sellers seemed to be asleep. I climbed to the top, up unspoilt cobbled streets to a park. It was green and cool. From here I could see two castles. I walked round one, or as much around as was possible, and looked out at the view. You get the feeling here that you can see all of Sicily below you – cultivated fields, green trees on the slopes, vineyards, bare beaches, promontories and white horses on the waves far out to sea. There's a cool breeze, but it's not windy.

The other castle contains the ruins of the temple. I sat on its steps waiting for it to open, eating a mess of figs from a squashed paper bag.

Just before three, an old man unlocked the gate. All that I could see inside was a dungeon or two and a well belonging to the castle. Near the well there were a few large white blocks in the ground – probably the foundations of the old temple. I took a minute fragment of marble to bring me luck in my future affairs. I expect centuries' worth of lovers have done the same and that's why there's no temple left. I also prayed to the goddess to get my beloved back for me and to make him more willing. Perhaps the prayer is beginning to work now . . .

There were a lot of couples wandering round the town, perhaps praying their own prayers. I've always found the Greek and Roman gods far more attractive than disapproving old Jehovah. I can tell he wouldn't like me. We haven't got much in common. You can't possibly pray to *Him* for things like that. It's quite against my nature to say *Thy will be done*. I can see why the Catholic Church has a lot of saints who can be prayed to for trivialities.

I returned to the bus regretfully. I'd have liked to spend longer. It's a place of great natural beauty, cool colours, green trees, grey buildings and white outcrops of marble in the ground. If you want a really good view, go up Eryx, not bloody Etna.

I took the train from Trapani back to Palermo. I had meant to visit Segesta, but was out of time. Besides, I had been put off by George MacBeth telling me that the famous Greek theatre there was populated by red spiders.

Giovanni

The Rome train proved to be a crowded one. Opposite me was Giovanni, an ancient lecherous taxi-driver over from New York. He had just been visiting his mother in the small town of Salemi. He was on his way to a villa he owned in Rimini. He kept insisting I talk to him in English so that the other people in the carriage didn't understand what we were saying. Of course he didn't want them to hear him trying endless persuasions to get me to go to his villa in wretched Rimini – somewhere that seems to have only a beach to recommend it. I was beginning to get the feeling I'd heard it all before. I was reminded of the sea-captain when he'd said he would put me up free and take me round and spend money on me. All he asked in return from '*his* women', he said, was that they 'love him a little'. Old men who think they should be *loved* in return for a little money ought to be kicked up the arse with steel-tipped jack-boots. I wished I'd had them with me.

To add to his other obnoxious qualities, Giovanni was racialist. 'You *want see* some *black people*?' he said contemptuously, tapping the open window within earshot of a passing African.

Giovanni had left his home-town to get work. He had himself been an immigrant for the last forty years or so, and yet he wanted *these* immigrants kicked out. Considering how long he'd spent in America his English was inexcusably lousy. I listened in to his conversations with the other Italians in the carriage. He was really enjoying himself boasting to a family which had emigrated to Belgium, but were now out of work. He kept saying he had made enough to retire young (not *all that* young, I thought), and that he had a flat in New York, a condominium in Florida and a villa at Rimini with a Mercedes in the garage.

He had once been a policeman in Rome and had a picture to prove it. Now he was returning for his annual viewing of the Sistine Chapel and the Trevi Fountain – just what any goddam tourist would see. He had turned into a pig of an American, in fact, without being able to speak the lingo. Like the worst tourists he had too much luggage with him – huge aluminium cases. The only Italian touch was a big thermos carrier of hot food that his mother back in his hated home-town had prepared for him.

Throughout most of the night, he dominated the carriage. We were all forced to look at pictures in a 3-D viewer. He had endless shots of Niagara – a bit trying when you have to climb over a carriageful of legs every time you want to pee. We were told too how beautiful Puerto Rico was – his other holidaying spot. Everybody had to agree. I stuck out on that one. I'm buggered if I'm going to admire tower blocks and tidal waves for anybody, least of all a prick like that.

I was quite glad of the diversions caused by the baby next to me on her Neapolitan mother's lap. Anna was a good baby. She only filled her pants once during the thirteen-hour journey to Rome. I gave her mother a spare paper bag to put the disposable nappy in. Giovanni chivalrously got up and threw it out of the window, contents and all. Anna had an insatiable appetite for pear juice and milky coffee. I assuaged her first crying fit with a little paper fan I'd had out of an ice cream in the mosquitoey restaurant of the night before. The two Belgianised Italian kids were better with her, though. I was a bit afraid to use much Italian on her in case I corrupted the pronunciation of her first words. All I felt like risking was a '*Che c'è?*' (What is it?) which I'd heard a lot of Italians say to their kids.

Anna was sensible enough to shut up with notice, pear juice, coffee or fans. Her mother was the paranoid one. She talked melodramatically of how she could only live for her child now, her life had been ruined. She had been a beauty with black hair, but marriage had finished her looks and turned her grey at twenty-two. She was worried that her husband in Palermo would look for other women now she had lost her looks. I'd seen him saying goodbye on the platform. He had quite a nice face – he might have been handsome once – but he was getting very thin on top. Giovanni gallantly told her she looked thirty-two, not twenty-two. Actually, she looked a good-looking forty. I suppose that marriage does age women, but nobody's life is ruined by age unless they give up on things.

Anna and mother got off at Naples to go and stay with their family. Giovanni told them that he would have driven them all the way to their house on the outskirts, if his Mercedes had not been in Rimini.

We all spread out when they'd left. I continued making a horrid spectacle of myself, cleansing my face repeatedly – something that had fascinated baby Anna but I thought would not fascinate Giovanni. I sat around covered in dollops of face cream, hoping he would not renew his offers of a free night in the Hotel Cardinal in the middle of Rome en route for Rimini, the Mercedes and *him*. He simply slapped on after-shave and looked inviting. When the train drew in I was off up the platform like greased lightning. I left my luggage in the deposit office and went to the Vatican. I had determined to get to Rome that day as the museums are free on the last Sunday of the month.

Toy Boys

I wanted to get a look at the newly restored bits of the Sistine Chapel. I had been told that Michelangelo's paintings are very colourful with the muck of years cleaned off. In fact, half of the ceiling is still covered with scaffolding. I wanted to see the sibyls in full technicolor. Only two have been done so far – Delphica and Erythraea. You can buy cards of them. They only sell cards of the cleaned bits on the bookstall. It's amazing how much younger these two sibyls look in their degrimed state – quite muscular and firm in flesh, more human and less ominous without all that greyness.

The buses from the Vatican area are always even more tightly packed than the others. I watched an Australian girl without much Italian chatting up a local boy in a vest with short hair spiked back with setting gel – I hate that fashion. She was trying very hard, which hardly seems necessary with an Italian. She fixed her date with him, tenderly fingering his spikes, or button-holing him by the vest. Was he married, she asked, after they'd agreed to meet at her hotel. Yes, he said, hesitating, but he didn't think a boy as young as he was should have to be faithful to one woman. That was for older men. I hadn't noticed.

There's not much open on a Sunday afternoon, so I thought I'd take to the Alban Hills. The train climbs steeply. After running through strange-looking country with odd, possibly Etruscan remains cut into cliffs, you come into the resorts. I got off at the end of the line, Albano, and tried various roads to find a strange Etruscan tomb that is supposed to lie just outside. Perhaps I'd have been luckier in a car. Various odd miles in various directions seemed to get me nowhere.

Albano has a few Roman remains – odd walls, a cistern and so on. It also has a large central park which seems to be constructed on a lap of the Appian Way, judging by the lofty, regularly-planted ancient pine trees there. The park specialises in romantic wedding photos of brides in long trailing gowns against a large bed of bright red flowers. There's a photographer's nearby and various brides were being done as I passed through.

The train back was filled with all the local yobboes, male and female, tarted up for a night out in Rome. It was then that I was chatted up by Gilbert and George, or rather Giorgio and Erico.

I had my name and the road I was staying in forced out of me by Giorgio, the ebullient one. They would take me for a pizza that night, they insisted. Hours later it turned out that they had the initiative to find my hotel, though I hadn't told them the name of it. Giorgio came giggling to my room. I said I needed half an hour to get ready and would meet them downstairs.

Erico was in the driving seat. Although I told them I'd seen the obvious things, I had to have the tourist tour and the view from the Pincian Hill, which I've seen before and was never thrilled by.

After we'd eaten at a touristy spot, I was driven back. Erico kept suggesting I suck him off while he was driving and trying to push my head in that direction. Giorgio howled with laughter on the back seat. Now I know why they all drive like that in Rome. Next time I'm nearly run down by a maniac there I shall assume that he has some more obliging tourist slumped across his crotch.

The proprietor of my hotel was gay, my companions told me before dropping me off. I think they hoped I'd take them upstairs when I heard that my needs could not be serviced by him. Boys who want to get lucky shouldn't hunt in pairs.

I had bought a book on the catacombs while I was in the Vatican that morning. It had a lot of good colour illustrations of frescoes in catacombs I had not seen. (As a lapsed Protestant with many generations of Calvinistic Methodist ancestors behind me, I shouldn't have trusted anything from such a source.) The next day, when I set out to look for them, I found that they were closed.

There are a number of entrances round the outskirts of Rome – things like police boxes or air-raid shelters or plain doors in walls – that lead down to the maze beneath. Many of the closed doors have little plaques telling you to apply to this or that cardinal, perhaps long dead, judging by the age of the inscriptions. Others tell you to get permission from the Archaeological Section at the Vatican. Maybe one day I will. The reproductions in the book seem to show some very good paintings, perhaps better ones than those on offer in the five open catacombs.

The only extra, open catacomb I found that day was beneath St Lawrence's. The catacomb is that of St Cyriaca – a woman saint I know nothing about. There's only an upper layer left here, beneath the church and the more modern cemetery nearby. The lower levels with their frescoes had now become too dangerous for visitors. Why on earth doesn't somebody get what's left of the paintings out and transfer them carefully to a museum? Rome is so rich in art I think it is sometimes careless about its early heritage.

These catacombs are not vastly interesting ones. There are still plenty of bits of bone around for those who collect relics as a hobby. My father once knew a gravedigger who lived in Cologne and sold 'relics'.

The cloister above is more worthwhile than this particular catacomb. It contains a lot of fragments of sarcophagi with admirably sculpted biblical scenes.

I felt bad, wasting a day when I had so little time left. I ought at least to pick somebody up to finish the evening with more style, I thought. I've always been a workaholic. I found myself a very young graphic designer at the station while I was trying my hand at the train information computers.

My toy boy turned out to have the rather historic-sounding surname *Flaminii*. I think that must have meant that he was descended from the *flamens*, the priests of ancient Rome. He lived outside in the Alban Hills.

That evening, I realised I'd landed the dirtiest talker in the world. He asked for endless comparisons for Italian swear words or sex words, most of which I had never heard of and unfortunately can't remember. The Italians still seem to have equivalents for extinct Elizabethan words like *whoreson*. He could hardly believe it, though, when I said that we had no expression like *porco di Dio*, or *porco di Madonna*. Still, I impressed him by saying that we sometimes call our policemen *pigs*. Evidently the Italians hadn't thought of that.

I was also told a lot of tales of Boccaccio-esque cuckoldry in a restaurant. I told him some English ones back, about people I knew at home, and made him scream with laughter. I was beginning to feel I was in the middle of a sixteenth-century jest book.

Were Englishmen all gay, he asked. Ah, my chance for revenge! I told him no, they were just cold. Did they make love in the same way as Italians? Yes, I said, but they didn't want to often. I'm only judging by my own experiences, of course. I've told quite a few Italians about English men being cold. I also tell them that the women are as strong as amazons and don't wear knickers.

In order to persuade me to have sex in his car in a park, my toy boy said that if I had a lover back home, I could pretend I was having it with him. I've never heard that self-annihilating argument before. It's not something I'd ever want to do – the substitute's performance might well not be up to the other and I might blame the wrong person.

The latter-day descendant of the *flamens* had a very Etruscan prick, I decided. An uncircumcised misshape, a second in Fate's lottery, just like the votive offerings in museums.

I searched the car floor for the top button of my blouse, which was missing. Inevitably, my partner made various jokes about where it could have disappeared, before tearing a button off his shirt and giving it to me as a replacement. The button turned up that night – not where he had thought, but in my hotel bedroom.

I had a strange offer when we parted – a correspondence course in Roman swearing. Rome has a lot of slang that is all its own. *Fare fiche a fiche* means mutual masturbation in Rome, sex else-where. (Or is it the other way around?) In Rome *la pipa* (ordinarily a pipe) is also masturbation, *la pompa* (a pump) – fellation. I thought long and carefully about it, but never took the correspon-dence course. I was afraid this young ebullient swearing Roman might turn up on my doorstep one day.

Etruscan Places

The next morning I left very early. I had to do several changes for the long journey to Volterra. First I took the Turin train for Grosseto, then a local one to Cecina, where I waited for a bus. Cecina has a thriving but fairly expensive market. The only cheap part here was the food. I stocked up on provisions and ate a *porchetta* roll. These are usually lightly spiced salted pork – this one though had whole chillies concealed – perhaps they shove them in for English customers. I got to the chillies by the time I was on the bus. Tears streamed from my eyes and I tried in vain to quench my mouth with several nectarines and a pint of tepid water. The old women in black on the bus looked on with interest.

There are trains to part of Volterra, but the line is obviously being run down and most of them are replaced by a bus which you use railway tickets for. The bus climbs through countryside until it leaves you at Volterra Saline – an area of farmland and salt-pits. To get to Volterra proper you wait an hour for another bus, having bought tickets at a nearby bar. If you set off from Rome at 8 or so, you will get there by the afternoon.

Volterra is a beautiful, small, walled town on top of a hill. There are Etruscan and Roman remains here and an exceptionally good museum. It's the sort of place you ought to stay at rather than pass through within a day, at the mercy of bad transport.

The museum contains an exceptionally large collection of small alabaster funeral urns. There must be several hundred of them. The curators have grouped them according to the scenes depicted on the sides. On the ground floor the most interesting examples of all are arranged.

The top of each casket is a sculpture of the deceased – a vivid portrait head, slightly under life-size on a reclining body in about half life-size proportion. The effect is extremely strange. It is definitely an effect that the artist intended because the figures sculpted on the sides show a high degree of skill in naturalistic representation. This museum, in other words, contains the most definite proof, running to hundreds of exhibits, that ancient artists intended their distortions quite as much as any modern ones.

It is a very frightening museum. When you look at the sides of the urns you see scenes of horror. The paintings in Tarquinia were serene in their view of death, but those were from an earlier, happier time. Most of these exhibits belong to the first or second century B C, a period when the power of the Etruscans was vanishing completely.

The ground floor contains the urns with depictions of the *Viaggi agli Inferi* – the Journey to the Underworld. There is nothing passive or willing about the victims. The faces shown reveal various degrees of fear or terror as they are dragged by demons. Tukulka often features amongst these demons. There are faint traces of colour left on the alabaster. Probably, he and the other demons were bluebottle-coloured as they are shown in the paintings of this period. Charun, the death-god, creeps up behind, with satyr-ears and a savage mask. He always carries a hammer as if he is about to crush their skulls in.

Curiously, the *dispater*, the man who dragged corpses out in the Roman Games, was always dressed like Charun. The Romans derived many rituals from the Etruscans. Candlemaking in all its forms was taken over from them. Lamps did not come in until 300 B C.

After Caesar's assassination the Senate called for seers from Etruria to interpret various portents. The eldest told them that kingly rule was coming back, and that they would all be slaves except for himself. He then held his breath until he dropped dead. It's a nice story. I feel however it's likely that the man only fainted dramatically, then had a good laugh at the Romans afterwards. I used to hold my breath at school – a faint got me out of lessons. I think it unlikely that anyone could kill themselves that way.

Knowledge of the language was preserved by soothsayers. The Emperor Claudius was particularly well-versed in this tongue and gave an address to the Senate about preserving Etruscan rituals. Other emperors had an Etruscan soothsayer or two in their entourage even in the latter days of Rome. Julian the Apostate was accompanied by hosts of them. Maybe they used Latin translations of the old ritual books. Perhaps, though, the Etruscan language still survived with them. The priestly office was hereditary in Etruscan noble families. The art of divination was reserved for nobles and their wives.

There were, it seems, several ways to go to hell – on foot, on horseback, in a chariot or covered wagon. The curators have meticulously classified their examples according to this, giving up a room, or part of a room to each type. My mind was taken back to Cerveteri, its empty tombs and the Via degli Inferi, so deeply rutted by the traffic of carts that it is hardly possible to walk along it. I thought also of the way the wagons of dead must have rolled through the sea across the underwater causeway from Motya to Birgi. Of those Phoenician rites even less is known. The finds on Birgi revealed little but superhuman-sized sarcophagi.

Upstairs in the museum, the scenes are less horrible on the surface. These are defined by the curators as mythological. When you look closely, though, none of the myths are gentle ones – all battles of centaurs, the Rape of Proserpine, etc.

As far as I could see, there was only about one urn in the place with a happy emblem on the side – a large decorative rose. This urn was not alabaster but tufa. Why did the woman whose remains were in it get off lightly? It's a mystery no one will ever be able to sort out.

There are a few happier exhibits – an ugly but contented couple on a sarcophagus and a plate with a *rappresentazione erotica*, as the Museo Guarnacci puts it. (The bloke is sitting on an animal and buggering or fucking from behind a woman half on his lap, half wrapped around a branch. I suppose it would be rather nice to have pottery like that and watch the face of the vicar as he took the last biscuit.)

There is something curiously modern about Etruscan art. Apart from the deliberate distortions of the figures on the urns, there is an unexplained BC Giacometti. He's not the only thin man in this museum. There's a reclining boy with pathetic legs like an Oxfam advert, tucked away upstairs. It is still painted red.

Downstairs, the bookstall sells paperbacks of D. H. Lawrence's *Etruscan Places*. A tempting wrapper says that it's by the author of *Lady Chatterley's Lover*.

I left the museum regretfully. It's the sort of place it would be nice to spend a week drawing in, just to try to begin to understand the minds behind those sculptures and their curious proportions.

I walked back to the bus stop and spent my last two minutes in a horrible sound and light show in the church of San Antonio Abate. It seemed more like hell than any Etruscan cemetery. Some smart arse had dissected a modern, rather bad picture of a Crucifixion. The screen showed detail after detail of it in a blacked-out church, to the accompaniment of crashing electronic chords. In the card shops nearby, Volterra makes its other ploy for tourist success – expensive art cards of statues' private parts. In deference presumably to German visitors, the restaurants have a lot of wild boar on the menu. Maybe it's caught in the thickets lower down the hill.

Romantics

My next intended stop was Mantua. A town named after the
Etruscan infernal deity Mantus, according to some, although Dante
states categorically that Virgil gave him another explanation, personally. My journey was a complexity of changes through the
night. Everyone I talked to about Volterra had been there, but told
tales of endless buses and missed connections.

Somewhere, some time after midnight I met an Albanian who
wanted to take me to Venice, but I was warned against him by a
toothy Italian girl heading home to Vicenza. Albanians haunt the
trains of northern Italy apparently in search of women. She told
me how beautiful her home-town was, which is something that
almost all Italians do wherever they come from. I left Vicenza and
its industry to her.

Mantua must be about the only place in Italy with bad water.
It tastes salty and polluted. The fruit is all dear too. A nice Yugoslav
woman I talked to coming over on the plane had told me that the
best local delicacy was pasta with stinging nettles, but I wouldn't
have known what to ask for.

I was there briefly to see the Mantegnas in the *Camera degli
Sposi* of the Ducal Palace. There was the long tour of the rest
before we got to these – long and wearing because we were forced
to keep with the guide and go at the speed of the slowest in the
party. Most of the paintings are too late to be of interest. The
earliest – the Pinturicchios – are terribly damaged, with pencil
outlines drawn on to suggest what might be. The only out-of-the-
ordinary things in that part were the little rooms you can see
through a window in the corridor that once housed the family's

dwarfs. The Mantegnas, when we got to them, were beautiful, with their strange *trompe l'oeil* effect. But after all the dawdling on the way, we were rushed in and out in minutes for fear our breath would alter the humidity in the room.

Before leaving Mantua I saw their fairly horrible statue of Virgil. Virgil was born there, although the citizens hadn't thought to commemorate this until comparatively recently. I also went to Mantegna's house, which survives intact and is used for modern art exhibitions. The present one was dedicated to Goethe. The paintings were by Edoardo Bassoli. He had used fluorescent paints. To prove they were fluorescent the lights went off occasionally. Poor Goethe, what had he done to deserve this portrait, half-purple, half-pink? There were a lot of orgasmic girls in the pictures. One entitled *In cuore mi penetra un fuoco* – a fire penetrates my heart – had a girl with lime-green nipples reclining near, between or on top of two blue lions with perms. There was a lot of pink in the other pictures. I walked into a wall and hit my nose at one point when the lights went off and the lime-green nipples didn't come up quick enough. Poor Goethe! Poor Mantegna! I went to catch my train.

I shopped briefly in Venice before heading back to Rome. As I waited for my train I was picked on by Jozip, an amorous Yugoslav who worked on the station. He was wearing a medallion of the Black Madonna which had come down in his family. I had nothing to worry about, he said, as he followed me on to my train – he was just *romantico*. He sang me a line or two of 'O Sole Mio', which made me snigger in his face. Faint heart never won fair lady. Nothing deterred, he pulled the curtains, closed the doors, etc., then got his cock out. I hit the bottom of the blind so that it flew up suddenly. I wanted the platform full of people to see what a good specimen he had. My *romantico* then took hold of my hand and said: 'Andiamo alla toiletta.' Now, I'm not romantic, but I have no intention of ever going to a toilet to do it. I know some people do.

In the morning I went to Orvieto. Like Volterra, it's a hill town of Etruscan origins. There are shops and modern buildings near the station, but the main part is a bus ride away. It's a prosperous little town in the middle of a wine-growing region.

The old quarter has many Medieval buildings. Coming away

from this you find a thriving market more or less in the centre of the town. There are plenty of visitors, but it's not nastily touristy. Ordinary life goes on.

The cathedral, the local English version tourist leaflet tells me, is the *Golden Lily of Cathedrals*. It is certainly an interesting one with its side-chapels full of Signorellis. The pictures are full of life in all its forms – skeletons, baby angels, sphinxes, satyrs – you name it, they've got it.

The paintings cover Resurrection, the Damned, the Elect and the History of Antichrist. There is much that reminds me of the morbidity of late Etruscan art. I once read a view that all the great colourists amongst Italian artists came from areas settled by the Etruscans. I haven't really gone into this, much as I have an urge to disprove all categorically stated theories. I think heredity does influence your style, but Europeans have moved around so much, from the Romans on, that it's hard to tell who might or might not be descended from the Etruscans. I can see this kind of influence in Giotto, Michelangelo and Signorelli, certainly. But then, there are curious similarities between the earlier happy Etruscan painting and the works of Matisse and Picasso. Perhaps Italian artists who deal with Death and the Damned have something in common with the late despairing sculpture of Volterra and the few fragments of demon frescoes elsewhere.

The Damned in the Chapel of San Brizio are being dragged or tied by strange livid-coloured winged demons quite out of the Christian tradition. In most of the Medieval accounts you read, devils and Negroes are equated. Mentioning an Ethiopian was enough. He didn't even need cloven feet. Signorelli's devils come in several kinds: the flying ones have short twisty horns and sturdy multi-coloured wings like Victorian fairies; others, halfway between men and spirits, have wild hair or floppy ears, strange hairy skins about their loins and bodies part green, part pinky-grey, part livid putrid blue-lilac. Some of these have short embryonic horns as if they are in the process of acquiring full demon status. The archangels standing on clouds in the sky are not doing too well against them. They are just like human knights with wings. In fact, they look too human to cope with what's below and around. In the middle, a woman with long blonde hair is being flown off on the back of a demon. She has that same look of fear that I saw on the coffers of Volterra. In a space between a window and the arch of the ceiling there is a painting of Charon and his boat, ferrying the souls brought by demons. There is very little colour in this part of the painting. The rocks and the boat are a dull brown. As far as I could make out, though, this was Charun, not Charon – a winged figure definitely. There are vignettes nearby amongst a mass of decorative figures. Empedocles looks out at the end of the world, Virgil peeps nervously while writing it up, Dante is too busy reading to care a tuppeny fuck.

The Elect are of course less interesting, like the *Paradiso* and *Paradise Regained*. Heaven has to be a very boring place. All the literature of the world is based on sins, if you begin to think about it. The description of the glassy sea and the Ancient of Days is very offputting in the Bible – like an ice-rink disco for old age pensioners. Christianity is a bit like having to try a competition for a prize you don't want to win. Save all your cornflake packets for five years and you might get a package holiday in Siberia. I looked at the Elect and thought how, if I gave up fucking, drinking, swearing and taking revenge on people – all the things I like – I too could stand amongst this crowd of several hundred naked people with wisps of coloured cloth across their whatsits and listen to the lumpish orchestra sitting eternally on clouds above.

The picture of the Stories of Antichrist is a bit beyond me. I have read odd prophecies about Antichrist – the sibyls did their share – but I find it hard to think of them in any coherent form. Antichrist has been variously identified with Nero, Claudius, Popes, the Turks, Mohammed, Gorbachev and others. The picture could as easily be a sort of pageant of the life of Christ, like that at Marsala, but this Christ-type figure on a pedestal is being prompted by a demon. The Frenchman who keeps the local photocopy shop could tell me what this all means, I'm sure. He said that he has worked out the name of the Antichrist who will come soon, on the basis of Nostradamus's prophecies. The figures in Signorelli's painting all wear Medieval dress apart from the Christs. It's as if everyone wants Antichrist to come in their own time. At the side of this picture there are two sombre watchers in black, surveying like Dante and Virgil, but these are Signorelli and Fra Angelico.

The three museums of Orvieto are near the cathedral. The one that belongs to the church is not particularly interesting – a room full of worm-eaten religious pictures mostly by inferior painters. Only some Signorelli panels, a Simone Martini and one by a sixteenth-century painter I'd not heard of, Antonio di Viterbo, stood out. The Museo Claudio Faino is better, but not particularly remarkable. There are some good Etruscan urns with animals figured on them, black pitchers with bird figures on top, a long sarcophagus with a fat slug of a man on it and a large warrior's head. The museum owner's coat of arms is included in the collection – in tapestry. It appears to be a stoat rampant under a crown.

The small new archaeological museum is more to my taste. They have transferred a couple of Etruscan tombs here – *Tomba Golini I* and *II* – and set them up as they were. The curator follows you round and switches on the light for you in these. The paintings are faded and damaged. Little but red pigment remains – that seems the most durable of all. If you block out the most damaged parts with a hand before your eyes, you can begin to see a scene of priests, ritual and sacrifice, obviously a vivid painting in its day. The Etruscan sense of spacing was always good.

Back in the town, with a little photocopied map from the tourist office, I tried to find the local tombs. The map clearly sited them where various shops and restaurants stood. Perhaps they still had something in their basements. Probably, though, everything was thoroughly excavated and packed away into museums like the Punic necropolis at Marsala.

Outside the town, more or less, I came to the Well of San Patrizio, which turned out to be very much worth a visit. It was built in the sixteenth century by Sangallo the Younger, commissioned by Pope Clement VII. The Pope had transferred his court to Orvieto when the *Landsknechte* were sacking Rome. The well was necessary to ensure the town kept its water supply even if there was a siege.

The old man at the top let me go down free. He was clocking off for lunch and offered me a ride back to the station as there wasn't a bus due for a while. It takes a long time even to get to the bottom of the well and up again. There are shallow spiralling steps curving round a central core which has windows all along the way. It is a double spiral in fact. It was built this way so that donkeys going to the bottom need not pass others coming up. I learnt this from one of the tourist phones on the wall that you can put 200 lire in. I could hardly believe it, so I watched out for a broken phone I'd noticed on the way back. There wasn't one, so presumably it's true. Sangallo must have been a very ingenious architect. The windows in the central part give access to the light from the top. It gets a lot darker on the way down though. The well is many storeys high. It's hard to count how many by the windows in the side, because the light gets in your eyes as you look up from the bottom – probably about eleven or twelve. I was interested to see as I stood on the little bridge across the water at the bottom that when you look up you can't see stars. I've never believed that you would be able to from the bottom of a well. It never sounded right.

I emerged eventually from the other exit round the back. The well has a circular building at the top with a grid for a roof. A fig tree has planted itself at the edge of this grid. When I went round the front I met the little old man. On the way to the station, he suggested some Etruscan tombs.

Etruscan tombs are a great place for trying to rape tourists. The man gets the girl to go in first to look round the dank little burying place and points out its unusual construction, the angle of the ceiling, etc. Then, while she is admiring the interior, he sits down on the steps with undone flies, blocking the narrow exit. Going round a man wedged in place and ready and waiting is impossible. You have to try to climb over, which could land you in a very tangled sexual position. As I tried to step across the old bastard's right shoulder, he whipped up my skirt and muttered 'Bella.' I walked briskly away from the tombs and he ran after me wanking. When he'd come on the ground, I had to take a lift back to the station, having deviated off the bus route too far to find my own way. Luckily, by then he had calmed down. It was a very silent ride.

I had run out of time on my last trip. I had to find my way to Verona that night to catch a plane the following day. I caught the first train to Florence, where I had to wait for another. The train was full of young boys showing off. I wished I'd picked up more words from the descendant of the *flamens*. I could only half understand them. One of them was telling a tale of how his girlfriend said she was too full to suck him off. She'd had a pizza, four sandwiches, a few sweets, an ice cream, so she couldn't manage anything else without being sick. The others were complaining that they had erections – they did that part in gestures – and that they would have to get all the way to Bologna before there was any hope of relief.

Florence was full of English, hardly an Italian in sight. The group of boys had gone off to catch their train to Bologna. Like the Ancient Mariner, the girl nearest me on the platform was regaling various English strangers with her tale. She went from person to person complaining about the other girl she'd been sharing a tent with: 'She's so mean!' she whined. 'I gave her half my mince pie, but she wouldn't give me any of her toffee crisp.' She looked as if she'd had far too many toffee crisps. I pretended to be Italian when she asked me for train info. As an ambassador and type of all my race I don't like to fraternise with all the other ambassadors on holiday.